I0031790

Equity in Practice
Transformational Training Resource

Njoki Wane
&
Larissa Cairncross

Nsemia

Copyright © 2013
All rights reserved.

This publication may not be reproduced, in whole or in part, by any means including photocopying or any information storage or retrieval system, without the specific and prior written permission of the publisher.

This book is sold subject to the condition that it shall not, by way of trade or otherwise, be re-sold, hired out, or otherwise circulated without prior consent from the publisher in any form of binding or cover other than that in which it is published and a similar condition including this condition being imposed on the subsequent purchaser.

First Edition: August 2013
Cover Design: Danielle Pitt
Layout Design: Kemunto Matunda

Published by Nsemia Inc. Publishers (www.nsemia.com); Oakville, Ontario, Canada

Note for Librarians: A cataloguing record for this book is available from Library and Archives Canada

ISBN: 978-1-926906-20-1 paperback

DEDICATIONS

Dedicated to the late Professor Roxana Ng
– CIARS Director 2003-2005

TABLE OF CONTENTS

SECTION TWO
EXERCISES

SECTION THREE

SECTION FOUR
Institutional Self-Assessment

Sources - 73

APPENDIX

ABOUT THE AUTHORS

Njoki Nathani Wane, Ph.D. is a Professor at the University of Toronto is the current Special Advisor for Gender Issues and the Director for the Centre for Integrative Anti-Racist Research Studies (CIARS). She was also the first director for the Office of Teaching Support (OTSO) at OISE/UT. She has been teaching in the Department of Humanities, Social Science, Social Justice Education (formerly Sociology of Equity Studies) at the Ontario Institute for Studies in Education (OISE), University of Toronto, since 1998. In 2009, she was one of the TVO Nominee for Best Lecturer, while in 2008 she received Harry Jerome Professional Excellence Award and in 2007 she won the African Women Achievement Award. For the last twenty years she has been researching, writing and teaching in the areas of Black feminisms in Canada & Africa, African indigenous knowledges, African women and spirituality.

For the last twenty years she has been researching, writing and teaching in the areas of Black feminisms in Canada, African feminisms, African indigenous knowledges, anti-racist education in teacher education, African women and spirituality, and ethno-medicine. She has published widely in journals and anthologies in the areas of African women and indigenous knowledge, Black Canadian feminisms; African women and spirituality, anti-colonial thought and ethno-medicine. Her co-edited books include *Spirituality, Education & Society: An Integrated Approach* (with Energy Manyimo & Eric Ritskes) and *The Politics of Cultural Knowledge* (with Arlo Kempf and Marlon Simmons) both published by Sense Publications in 2011; *Theorizing Empowerment: Canadian Perspectives on Black Feminist Thought* (with N. Massaquoi), was published by Inanna Publications in 2007. Other recent publications include: Wane, *Reading Fanon Differently: Black Canadian Perspectives*. In George Dei (Ed) *Fanon and the Counterinsurgency of Education* (2010). Wane & Sutherland (2010) *African and Caribbean Indigenous Healing Practices and their Relevance to Counselling and Psychotherapy: Research Findings from Kenya & Grenada.* In Moodley & Anthony George. *Alternative Counseling & Healing.* Wane, N. Traditional Healing Practices: Conversations with Herbalists in Kenya. (2010) In Dip Kapoor & Edward Shizha. In Contemporary Asian and African Indigenous Knowledge and Learning: Essentialisms, Continuities and Change. Malgrave MacMillan. Indigenous Education and Cultural Resistance: a Decolonizing Project (2009), *Curriculum Inquiry*; Black Canadian Feminism Thought: perspectives on equity and diversity in the academy. *Journal Race Ethnicity and Education.* 12 (1). 65-77 (2009): and Mapping the Field of Indigenous Knowledge in Anti-Colonial discourse: A Transformative Journey in Education. *Journal of Race, Ethnicity and Education.* Vol 11 No.2. (2008).

Larissa Cairncross has worked since the 1980s as a researcher and consultant on equity, diversity, and anti-oppression projects in Toronto. Her experience in the South African anti-apartheid movement and work as part of a community-based research team contributed to the creation of the first African-centred service agency in Toronto, the *African Training and Employment Centre.* From 1989-1993 she was executive director of the agency as it became a key resource for the support and development of the expanding African communities in Toronto. As a consultant she developed a variety of training programs and materials for local and provincial government departments including *The Cultural Interpreter Training Manual.* She has an undergraduate degree in English literature and political science from the University of Toronto's Victoria University, and an MI (Master of Information) from the UT Faculty of Information school (2012).

FOREWORD

As societies become more diverse the educational discourse must be positioned with urgency to foreground issues of diversity and equity in theory, research and practice. Transforming society and the educational agenda to respond to needs of a growing diverse population is one of the important issues of education training today. Creating spaces in our workplace or schools where we can examine and reflect on issues of equity and diversity is important not only at an individual level but a societal level. In doing so we are taking into consideration the diversity and richness of experiences of our growing diverse population. As trainers, facilitators and coaches, we prepare members of our society with different ways in which they can engage with this new reality. We can no longer simply tell them what they should do; we have to provide training, resources and support to aid in self-transformation and repositioning of self to see diversity as an asset and not a liability. In business it is important for employers to master ways to respond in positive and productive ways to their increasingly diverse clientele and that is what this training resource is meant to do. It provides resources and examples that can be used in classrooms or workplaces in preparing staff for diversity training.

On the educational front, in the present cacophony of educational discourses we must resist reducing educational achievement to scores on a test, and redirect the focus through research and action to the benefits of authentic learning experiences that value the diverse experiences of students and challenge existing power arrangements, norms and practices. As the teaching staffs in schools continue to be white and middle class, their experiences and socialization are often in dissonance with their students. Much of the data on teaching profession show that while the demographics of the students are changing rapidly the demographics of the teaching staff remain the same. This is also evident in the teacher candidate pool in many faculties of education where teacher candidates are also predominantly white, female and middle class. Some faculties of education and universities have undertaken outreach activities to attract those groups traditionally unrepresented, but progress is slow.

This reality makes a training resource on equity an imperative. If and when business are to become *equity-lived*, meaning they actively engage in critical pedagogies and actions that foreground the lived experiences of diverse students and populations, embed equity in their daily practices, move from what I call *comfort-equity* to *critical equity* we must provide strategies that support a transformative educational agenda that build new knowledge grounded in an understanding that views diversity and equity as assets and provide spaces that can wrestle with the tensions on the journey recognizing what they need to learn and unlearn. For example, we must provide strategies that assist teachers, employers, and employees in developing ways to interact with diverse populations. For teachers specifically, they must be supported in recognizing how their identities are taken up in the classroom and read by students and how this affects the teaching and learning process. Dr. Wane et. al. have undertaken the difficult task of writing a training manual on equity that can be used not only in school spaces, but the workforce as well. This equity training resource provides an excellent analysis of the history and social context of racism and other forms of discrimination as well as an examination of multiculturalism from a critical perspective. The questions and exercises in this resource are thoughtful and well illustrated and can be used by teachers in K-12 classrooms as well as facilitators and trainers in businesses. The activities in this manual will be of benefit both to practitioners and researchers in teasing out ways that equitable practices can become embedded in their everyday work. The resource encourages readers to reflect on the following crucial questions: To what extent are we responsible for the creation and implementation of experiences that promote positive growth not only at an individual but also at an institutional level? What happens when we feel that issues of equity and diversity speak only to a particular segment of our society? How are we affected by issues or race, gender, sexual orientation, religion, language, age, and ability? Readers will find this training resource useful and informative in creating critical praxis towards a more equitable education for all.

Ann Spence-Lopez, Ph.D.
Ontario Institute for the Studies in Education
University of Toronto
Toronto, Ontario
May 31, 2011

INTRODUCTION

> The reality is that Canadians of all origins have always been aware
> of racism and its effects within our society. It is not possible for a
> person to indulge in racist behaviour without the moral responsibility
> of acknowledging consciousness of the fact....When attitudes and acts
> of racism are enshrined in institutions invested with social or political
> power the victims are effectively marginalized. (Frederick Case, *Racism
> & National Consciousness* (2002: 36).

As we start the first decade of the twenty-first century, we still face monumental challenges around race and its impact on our education systems. Our education curricula, which ideally should reflect the multicultural faces and realities of our society, both past and present, continue in great measure to ignore the contributions of the diverse peoples who helped shape Canada. Progress is indeed coming, but at an incredibly slow pace. Three initiatives are essential toward redressing the imbalance: (1) concerted development of professionalism among all educators including teachers, facilitators, trainers and instructors so that they bring a transformational ethos into the learning environment, (2) a substantive review of curricula as currently exist; and (3) inclusion of unvarnished historical *truth* in our political, social, and education historical texts. Admittedly, over decades there have been a stream of governmental print (provincial and federal) that recognize the essentiality of these factors, but if the goal is genuine change to current processes, behaviours, and policies that underpin existing exclusionary ideologies and consequent practices, we as educators must also strive to be more pro-active in the pursuit of equity.

The authors of this manual concede that much of the foregoing is pretty much understood and accepted by transformational-directed educators working in today's educational system. But questions remain: To what extent are we responsible for the creation and implementation of experiences that promote positive growth, not only at an individual but also at an institutional level? What happens when we feel that issues of equity and diversity speak only to a particular segment of our society? How are we and our students or participants affected by issues of race, gender, sexual orientation, religion, language, age, and ability?

Equally salient, what do we *mean* by equity? Is it the same as equality? How much do we know about these categories of difference? What do we *really* think and feel when issues of equity and diversity are raised? Are we interested in exploring such issues further? Do these issues have meaning in our lives?

A self-reflective process is necessary for each of us as teachers, facilitators, trainers and instructors, and how we answer such questions is critical to our understanding of practices that should be fundamental in any society that desires to advance multiculturalism beyond cultural tokenism.

The **Equity in Practice Manual** is directed at those who desire to embark on a process of self-transformation, and also meant to serve as a motivator for teachers, facilitators, trainers, instructors and pre-teachers who want to begin or continue practices aimed at ensuring that the diversity of the learning environment is acknowledged in both theory and practice. Classroom 'norms' as currently exist are not truly 'normal'. According to Carson & Johnson (2000), the encounters of multiculturalism are bound to have profound effects on how educators engage with issues of diversity. Society cannot truly take credit for being diverse if this diversity is ignored within schools and workshops whose very purpose is to educate the country's children and the workforce, and indeed many adults, about Canada, the world, and themselves.

The manual is not intended to provide an answer to every complex problem, but rather to help begin the process that will remind us of our humanity as we educate and engage 'others' who may be 'different'.

ABOUT THE *EQUITY IN PRACTICE* MANUAL

The manual provides a training framework to aid educators including teachers and pre-service teachers in their understanding of the issues surrounding a complex education and social problem. In addition, the manual will be very useful for staff development in organizations, community colleges, and workplace training. It could be adopted by facilitators leading staff development and faculty using the exercises in their classes and workshops. It could also be adopted for students who are training to be peer facilitators, Inter-group Dialogue leaders, and Residence Hall Advisors. In summary, the manual is directed towards those who lead (or are being trained to lead) classes and workshops.

Section One provides historical information and theoretical discussions on the origins of racism, as well as the resistance to racism in Canada through reviews of its social context, government responses (starting with the initial policy of multiculturalism) and the subsequent and ongoing forms of anti-racist work. Section Two consists of a series of consciousness and skills-building exercises intended to be delivered and guided by trained facilitators only. Many of these exercises may elicit volatile responses, and learning is generally optimized through a process managed by an experienced trainer.

Traditionally, educators have been prepared to teach from a curriculum of sameness. In this regard, Carson & Johnson (2000) state that "[t]he curriculum of teacher education has been traditionally structured around an array of commonalities of normal child development, learning theories, provincially mandated programs of studies, instructional planning procedures, and the identification and measurement of expected outcomes (1)." Given this, what can we say about diversity in the preparation of diversity trainers? This question is central in the manual. We are conscious of diversity in our communities, and it is this consciousness that we find some educators unwilling to embrace. In addition, we make a concerted effort to explore a wide range of key aspects of diversity as taken up in various communities.

> In transformational approaches, education is part of a movement for individual and collective liberation, which promotes learning for critical consciousness and collective action. Arnold, Burke et al. *Educating for a Change* (p. 22).

THE CENTRE FOR INTEGRATIVE ANTI-RACISM STUDIES (CIARS)

The Centre for Integrative Anti-Racism Studies at the University of Toronto is, to our knowledge, the first in Canada devoted to anti-racism studies in education. Housed in the Department of Sociology and Equity Studies (SESE) at OISE, the Centre focuses on research that examines education from an integrative perspective, that is, education as a process embedded within wider social spheres. In 2002, the Centre organized a national conference on critical race scholarship which brought more than 300 participants together to present and debate their research on race and racism. At the conference, some of the most original thinking available on these subjects generated discussions that advanced our understanding of how the dynamics of racism in Canada are manifested.

In 2005, acute concern about the persistence of racism in education and the lack of sustained attention to this fundamental problem led to the Centre organizing a one-day "Teach-In." This event brought teachers, trainers, parents, and students together to share their experiences as seekers of education within Toronto schools, with teachers and student-teachers giving accounts of their experiences of being and becoming providers in teacher-education programs. From 2007 CIARS has also been holding Decolonizing the Spirit Annual Conference that has attracted over 200 participants each year.

In keeping with CIARS' goal of contributing to the production of alternative knowledge of racism in education, these projects have advanced a wider understanding of the underlying factors that created and maintain the acute symptoms of racialized tension within the educational system and the wider social environment.

The integrative approach employed by the Centre recognizes the intersecting forms of inequality. Additionally, this approach critiques the role of power in the perpetuation of racism, and criticizes racialized inequalities (Walcott, 1990, quoted by Raby, 2004). Based on these arguments, the authors suggest that educators need to address issues of educational equality, equity, and social justice not as mere add-ons, but rather as integral to the teaching and learning professions. These issues should encompass historical, cultural, religious, legal, and socio-political perspectives – crucial fundamental information if educators are to gain appropriate insight into the mores of learners, and become better equipped to eliminate the attitudes, perceptions, stereotypes and misconceptions they may currently have about students or participants and peoples from particular cultures. It is not enough to say that 'they', the 'Other', in becoming Canadian must adopt the culture of their new land. Indeed, as the fabric of multiculturalism in Canadian society continues to be woven with the threads of ever-growing and diverse cultural groups, the authors emphasize that any analysis of race must delve deeper into the reality of racial discrimination, oppression, and the socially-constructed concept of 'race'.

Raby (2004) writes that this deconstructing exercise requires a discussion of history that is "not simply a listing of racial injustices of the past, but history of the creation of race as a concept, ideological and imperial investments that were behind the construction of race and shifts in these constructions over time" (380).

Racism takes different forms and lends itself to acrobatic verbal manipulations. Mensah (2002), in distinguishing adjuncts to individual and systemic racism, states that there are two other forms of racism that are becoming increasingly popular in Canadian literature are new racism and democratic racism. The term 'new racism' is traced to the work of Martin Barker (1983) who describes it as a form of racism that is highly sophisticated and disguised through semantic manipulations. Unlike the old-fashioned racism, which relies on notions of innate biological superiority of Whites, new racism does not take such an extremist stance. It abandons such explicit racial language in favour of code words and race-neutral rhetoric. The works of Perera and Pugliese (1997) and Omi and Winant (1986) suggest that neoconservatives in the United States, Canada, Australia, and elsewhere in the West tend to *rearticulate* the meaning of concepts such as colour-blindness, racial equality, and race neutrality in ways that are disadvantageous to visible minorities. The new connotations accorded these concepts by the new right movement tend to disregard the historical and structural overtones of racial inequalities.

Thus our responsibility as educators is to be aware of the subtleties of racism, and go beyond confronting incidences of discrimination and address how oppressive situations continue to be constructed, deceptive, and ultimately executed. We also must acknowledge both visible and invisible sites of oppression. Some forms of diversity may not be visible (religious belief, disability, ethnicity, sexual orientation). Despite their invisibility they may affect learning and teaching just as strongly as more apparent diversity issues. The current educational environment is rife with situations that challenge the potential for a collective "peaceful enjoyment" of the achievements and privileges of those living in Canada. There are innumerable examples of harassment of racialized individuals and groups, and students within Ontario schools and, indeed, in school and after-school environments throughout Canada. The authors invite readers to examine the *Policy and Guidelines on Racism and Racial Discrimination* by the Ontario Human Rights Commission (9 June 2005), available at http://www.ohrc.on.

Within the educational environment, tensions surrounding equity issues all too often exist within any department of the academy. Beyond the academy, even into the workplace, continuing violence against Black youth by Metro police is a reality, and not to be ignored is the life-threatening disregard for the human and civil rights of members of communities arbitrarily targeted as security threats. Added to this unpleasant truth are the problems First Nations peoples face during encounters with multinational corporations who desire to appropriate Indigenous lands.

Media and other information sources (such as school curricula) perpetuate a climate of racial marginalization through omission of facts that contradict comfortable 'national' views and the privileging of dominant classes. It is within this atmosphere that social justice advocates struggle to generate useful alternatives and forms of resistance. CIARS focused its resources last year on developing the *Equity in Practice Manual* to serve as both a guide to antiracist information and as a training methodology. With this tool, the authors hope to contribute to an informed process of skills and knowledge-building among student and teacher groups and other trainers, facilitators, and instructors outside the teacher training programs. Thus, the manual will serve as a starting point for consciousness raising and transformative learning on issues of equity, racism, and decolonizing practice.

SECTION ONE

BACKGROUND TO RACISM IN CANADA

A review of history shows that racism became a focus of community activism and governmental policy in Canada from the mid-70s, particularly in the major urban centres of Toronto and Montreal. Numbers of visibly 'different' immigrants began to challenge the capacity of existing institutional and administrative systems to accommodate a variety of their needs. In 1995, *Currents,* the quarterly journal of the Urban Alliance on Race Relations (UARR), published a review of the preceding twenty years' work in race relations in Toronto by a disparate range of analysts. These analysts noted that while several successful campaigns had been mounted over the twenty years studied, problems of racism in Toronto had not merely continued, but had escalated. The key factors noted were that acts of racism were repeatedly minimized as ignorance, insensitivity, or isolated incidents (Henry, 1995: 13); systematic racism was denied through the logic of colour-blind democracy; and the forms of racism have changed. Today, the situation can be described in almost the same terms. The 5 July 2007 annual report of the Ontario Human Rights Commission documents an ongoing trend: "Racism persists in the old overt ways as well as in new and varied forms" (HR Commissioner Barbara Hall, quoted in 'Racism, bias, persist: Report', *Metro* article 6 July 2007, p. 6). Anti-racism advocates, trainers, and organizations have multiplied, but there is no shortage of grievances, inequities and outrages to keep them busy.

Although some issues continue to be present in much the same form – such as the lack of representative staffing in institutions – others have morphed into new and, in many cases, more violent and more sophisticated forms. A case in point is the recently amended Safe Schools Act which, while ostensibly intended to protect the in-school population, was in practice utilized most often to isolate and exclude students in a discriminatory pattern. A current research project to examine "systematic racism in the education system" identifies four areas of concern:

1. Employment Equity, where managerial-level employees of the Toronto District School Board and the Catholic District School Board do not reflect community diversity.

2. Curriculum, where elementary and secondary curricula do little to reflect the rich diversity in Toronto, and in some instances contain

material inherently offensive to one or more groups.

3. ESL-D/Heritage Classes, where ESL services and heritage language programs have been cut back, limiting the educational services available to students and putting their education at risk.

4. Safe Schools Act, where students of racialized groups are suspended in disproportionate numbers for "disciplinary infractions."

Although specific manifestations of these issues may reflect contemporary times, some versions have been identified and challenged for well over 30 years.   This environment impacts current and future students of the academy—the eventual educators in the system—through a cycle showing little sign of being fundamentally disrupted. There is continued confusion, lack of knowledge and skills, resulting in frustration and the inability to deal with situations that manifest underlying inequities. Such situations are a daily reality. "How can we change or disrupt assumptions about who belongs and what different people are like, ideas formed when racial equality was taken for granted, ideas which are so ingrained in people's minds?" (Wane, 2007: 3).

Confronting these problems, and rupturing entrenched practices was the impetus for the Centre for Integrative Ant-Racism Studies (CIARS) to undertake the current project of developing material, training, and other interventions that would contribute to building a more informed and appropriately-skilled teaching and leadership population.

However, even as we endeavour to promote a more transformative direction for teachers and diversity trainers who have the courage to become 'front line' advocates for genuine change, we cannot ignore the impact of privileged Canadian society, a society that unquestionably has proven resistant to true transformation.

The fundamental thought should be that we are all human beings living together in Canada and that every act, every word, even every attitude of mind will have repercussions with our society. Our first duty is to the building of a harmonious society in which a dynamic respect of the human dignity of the other is the focal point.

Case, *Racism & National Consciousness*, 2002: 52.

Social Context

The Canadian educational system has long been identified as having structural features that impose and maintain inequities. These inequities have educational, social, psychological, and economic consequences for those adversely affected and parallel benefits for those privileged by the same structural assumptions and exclusions.

The 1992 Ontario Ministry of Education's 'Resource Guide for Antiracist and Ethnocultural-Equity Education' described the situation as follows: "Ontario schools have been populated by students from a variety of backgrounds, but the school system...has been primarily Western European in content and background....As a result some students...have not seen themselves represented positively. The failure of the system to give equal attention and respect to all has contributed to stereotyping of some groups" (quoted in James, 1995, p. 37). The impact went much further than stereotyping. It included streaming into basic level programs, high dropout and failure rates, and low rates of post-secondary enrolment, particularly for Indigenous and Black students (James, 1995, p. 36).

An information sheet published by the Canadian Race Relations Foundation (CRFF) states: "[R]acism remains an imposing barrier to the equal access of racial-minority and Aboriginal students to educational achievement" (*Racism in Our Schools*, 2001, p. 1).[i] A discussion on CBC radio presented statistics revealing a 50 percent high-school dropout rate for Indigenous students in Ontario, rising to 75 percent in northern Canada. As Wane recently noted, "It is also common knowledge that preparing teachers for culturally diverse classrooms raises many difficult questions for teacher education....I am very conscious of diversity within our communities and it is this consciousness that I find some students unwilling to embrace." (Wane, 2007: 1)

Other critical analyses of the educational sector's culture, curricula, and models highlight hegemonic characteristics, among them:

- Anglo-Canadian culture presented as the "native" norm ("our home and native land")
- Settler history presented as a pioneering, groundbreaking enterprise in a *terra nullius* landscape

---

i   http://www.crr.ca/divers-files/en/pub/faSh/ePubFaShRacScho.pdf (accessed April 2007)

- English presented as a privileged language with French as the only other recognized partner in valued language skills

- Curriculum content that claims all North American and European achievement as original, self-generated, and self-financed

- Curriculum content that excludes positive images of racialized contributors involved in the creation of the modern Canadian state.

Expanding our perspective, we can locate the mindset of European hegemony which lies at the foundation of curricula content. Blout (1998) states, in this regard, that the "elite groupings of European countries together, in spite of their cultural (and national) differences, are a basic and permanent belief holding group, and their beliefs form, to a large extent, a single ethnography and ethnoscience....[T]hey have together underwritten the production of a coherent belief system about the European world, the non-European world, and the interaction between the two" (quoted in Graveline's *Circle Works*, 1998: 32). This belief system, though exclusive, Eurocentric, and clearly serving conqueror and settler interests, has been disseminated as a universal, impartial, unquestionable sociology to be accepted as common-sense for and by all.

Although there have always been resistance and justice-seeking responses from affected communities in Canada–notably the determination of Indigenous peoples to defend their rights and maintain their original relationships to the land, and the struggles of racialized populations such as the Black and Chinese communities to gain equal treatment alongside their White colleagues and fellow citizens – discrimination based on race, ethnicity, citizenship status, and other identity issues have not abated. A study released in October 2007[i] on the widespread practice of racial profiling recounts the experiences of Canadians from Muslim and Arab backgrounds whose human and constitutional rights have been violated, exposing them to random suspicion, arbitrary arrest, interrogation, and often deportation (in some infamous cases, to torture in their countries of origin or prior residency) under legislation introduced after 11 September 2001 (pp. 155-173). However, some may argue that heightened security issues dictate stern measures if Canada is to keep its citizens safe. In a story by CBC news on the website: http://www. cbc.ca/canada/story/2002/09/05/discrimination020905.html, last

---

i Smith, Charles. (2007). *Conflict, Crisis, and Accountability: Racial Profiling and Law Enforcement in Canada.* Canadian Centre for Policy Alternatives, Ottawa

updated Saturday, September 7, 2002, it is noted that "the Canadian branch of Council on American-Islamic Relations (Cair-Can) released the results of an informal survey ....About 60 per cent of the roughly 300 Muslims polled felt they were the targets of hatred by fellow Canadians. About 33 per cent said they were worse off since last fall's tragedy, while 39 per cent said the event had not changed their lives very much. The survey is considered unscientific because of its small sample size, but comments by individual Muslims ...underscored that discrimination is considered a problem in the Islamic community."

It is not the intent of this manual to take a position on state security, but rather to expose what may be a significant question: What was the climate in Canada regarding Muslims *before* the odious 11 September 2001 attacks on the World Trade Center Towers? This, the authors believe, is a more pertinent question because the rapidity with which the Islamic community was targeted and condemned may indicate a covert bias waiting for overt expression and seeming justification. Perhaps each of us should question our individual feelings and attitudes regarding members of the Islamic faith (and even the faith itself) because the answer is crucial to teaching and learning when we enter classrooms that have Muslim students or workshop participants. However, the government's foray into the Muslim community, whether considered justified or not, does indicate the prerogatives of power. When we also examine the ongoing harassment of Black males of all classes, ages, and appearance, these uses of state power have created an environment of mistrust and violence that has rapidly become normalized across the Canadian landscape. In its examination of racial profiling, CBC News Online, 25 May 2005 (cbc.ca.news/background/racial_profiling/) states: "A study of police statistics in Kingston, Ont., released in May 2005 found that young Black and Aboriginal men were more likely to be stopped than other groups. The data showed that police in the predominantly white city were 3.7 times more likely to stop a Black than a Caucasian, and 1.4 times more likely to stop an aboriginal person than a white.... The Association of Black Law Enforcers, an organization that represents black and minority police and law enforcement officers in Canada, says racial profiling exists."

Is it possible that many Black and Aboriginal males attending high school, college or university may have been either in the past or more recently the target of such profiling, or have been present in a vehicle when their father or older brother was such a target? Is it possible that this may affect how they react to White teachers in the educational system?

Racism and discrimination place a heavy load on those oppressed by bigoted and biased behaviours, whether motivated by gender, religious affiliation, sexual orientation, colour or ethnicity. As educators, we must be aware of the realities that daily confront our students, trainees and workshop participants. Being an effective educator requires the willingness to negotiate complex personal, social, and educational situations fostered by an admittedly complex world.

For the past 30 years, a variety of efforts have sought to combat the policies and social assumptions that generate and maintain systemic barriers and attitudes. These impediments make it possible for some Canadians to be regularly subjected to discrimination and violence of all kinds, based solely on the values ascribed to their 'differences' from the dominant norms.

MULTICULTURALISM IN CANADA

> Multicultural education singles out students and unintentionally facilitates the development of cultural, racial, ethnic, or religious stereotypes...by not delving in depth into the critical aspects of cultures, customs and histories. It is education in form rather than content.
>
> Volgyi, 2006: 11

Multiculturalism refers to a society of people of different cultural backgrounds, races or heritages. The Canadian society, for instance, reflects a vast diversity of cultural heritages and racial groups. This diversity is a result of centuries of immigration[i]. Before examining multiculturalism as governmental policy and how it is exhibited in Canadian society, we very briefly examine some aspects of what we mean by *culture*. This understanding is essential in teaching and learning, processes which in a multicultural environment require effective cross-cultural communication. Equally important to this understanding is what is meant by *Canadian* culture, for this lies at the core of curricula as currently exist.

Culture

"Culture has been defined in many ways—from a pattern of perceptions that influence communication to a site of contestation and conflict. Because there are many acceptable definitions of culture, and because it is a complex concept, it is important to reflect on the centrality of culture in our own interactions....How we think about culture frames our ideas and perceptions" (Martin & Nakayama, 2004, 2007, p. 81).

Indeed, it is how we frame these ideas and perceptions about race, ethnicity, class, gender, and sexual orientation that impact teaching and learning in the classroom. Although there are studies that enable an understanding of cultural differences between diverse ethnicities, it is crucial that as educators committed to transformational approaches we expand our views regarding these differences if intercultural communication is to be optimized.

Suderman (2007), with regard to a working *definition* of culture, references Benedict (1935) who states that "Culture is a set of learned patterns of thought and behaviour shared and passed down by a group of people. It consists of traditions, beliefs, values, norms, and symbols,

i *http://www.mta.ca/about_Canada/multi/*

the meanings and importance of which are shared in varying degrees by members of the community. Culture includes material and artistic objects (artifacts) created and used by the group." (p. 63)

Thus, culture is essentially a process of beliefs, practices and traditions inculcated through family and state, and includes art, food, religion, language, and a sense of identity. These things are a vital part of our histories, necessitating our understanding of how intercultural *difference* and *histories* are antecedents to effective communication. Thus, some questions arise: To what extent do cultural stereotypes and myths impact our role as teachers? What role does Canadian culture play within the classroom context? In fact, what is Canadian culture? The answers to these questions require self-reflection, and are essential to a transformational educator who desires sincere interaction with participants.

Canadian Culture

Although it is neither practical nor possible to be exhaustive in this manual with regard to Canadian culture, it can be said that as with that every country or nation, Canada is a product of history, politics, language, religion, and geography. And without question, history, politics, and language have rooted Canada's culture in British (Anglophone) and French (Francophone) traditions. We see the influence of First Nations in a wide variety of place names and names of rivers, so much so that they have become an indelible (geographical) part of Canadian culture. Canada has also been influenced by the influx of immigrants over the past 100 years, an immigration trend that continues to expand the population annually. As noted in the 2006 Census, *Portrait of the Canadian Population,* "The Canadian population grew more rapidly between 2001 and 2006 (+5.4%, representing a growth of 1.6 million) than in the previous intercensal period (+4.05). This acceleration was due to an increase in international migration." (5, 7)

Canada is a settler nation, both historically and currently as we recognize the continuing immigration of peoples from all over the world who, similarly to their counterparts (trappers, traders, pioneers) in the 18th century, still leave their lands of birth for the 'New World'.

Not to be overlooked is the influence of its southern neighbour which cannot be discounted. Myriad elements have combined to form what today may be called a *multicultural culture.* Education, particularly in Anglophone Canada, derives from a British culture embedded with Eurocentric worldviews and philosophies.

Suderman (2007), in looking at the common legacies of the United States and Canada, offers this insight: "The British colonial heritage provided the essential values, beliefs, and cultural patterns common to both nations. The dominant cultures of both were originally white, Anglo-Saxon, Protestant (WASP) elites that defined and controlled their political, social, linguistic, and commercial development of the British North American colonies both before and after their independence" (94). Both cultures were influenced by the Protestant Reformation, which emphasized the value of the individual (with racial and religious exclusion), the rule of law, and the value of work." (95)

Today, with solid arts, literature, science, and media pillars, Canada has evolved into a more multicultural nation than its founders possibly never imagined. This has brought to the cultural table worldviews hitherto undreamed of by those founders, resulting in a multicultural heritage enshrined in Section 27 of the Canadian Charter of Rights and Freedoms. However, it often seems that multiculturalism (more of it below) within the Canadian context signifies, albeit unspoken, the expectation that immigrants, no matter their original culture, assimilate a national identity based on the British colonial heritage. Some may argue that this is a natural and reasonable expectation. For, why would one desire to become Canadian and yet not want to adopt Canadian cultural values and mores? This argument is alluded to in a revised 16 March 2006 Parliamentary Information and Research Service (PIRS) document titled *Canadian Multiculturalism*, in which is stated: "The fear that the multiculturalism policy is promoting too much diversity at the expense of unity has been voiced increasingly in recent years. Critics say the policy is divisive because it emphasizes what is different, *rather than the values that are Canadian* (italics the authors'). Canadian culture and symbols, it is felt, are being discarded in an effort to accommodate other cultures. On the other hand, defenders of Canada's approach to multiculturalism argue that it encourages integration by telling immigrants they do not have to choose between preserving their cultural heritage and participating in Canadian society. Rather, they can do both." (6)

But what are the complexities of an identity involved in "doing both?"

As noted in the Introduction of Unit Seven, Double Bind: Canadian Identity, in *Pens of Many Colours* (ed. Eva C. Karpinski, 1997), "[T]he 'double bind' of Canadian identity consists of several paradoxes. For many Canadians, especially those with recent experience as immigrants or a strong ethnic identity, belonging to two cultures can be either enriching or bewildering (269)....If their cultural identity is more ethnic than Canadian, people may feel stigmatized and isolated from their community; if it is more Canadian, they might be estranged from their roots....If people cannot identify with either culture (or both cultures) strongly—or are rejected by both as 'inadequate'— they might feel lost in the ambiguous 'no man's land' between the two cultures" (270).

These are the paradoxes of 21st century Canadian culture and, as also noted in the Introduction to Unit Seven, "This 'cultural schizophrenia,' for some Canadians, persists as long as discrimination and stereotyping force us into definitions we refuse to identify with. On the other hand, feeling at home in both, one, or neither of the cultures seem to be a condition of living in Canada that we cannot—indeed, may not wish to—resolve" (271).

So we have yet more questions to address: What is really meant by multiculturalism? How does multiculturalism relate to Canadian culture or identity? To what extent does multiculturalism 'resolve' issues of discrimination and stereotyping? Or does it 'resolve' them at all? Let us briefly examine multiculturalism within the Canadian context.

Multiculturalism

The policy of "multiculturalism within a bilingual framework" was introduced by the federal government in 1971 and codified in the 1988 Multiculturalism Act. While the Act acknowledged the "diversity of Canadians as regards race, national or ethnic origin, colour and religion as a fundamental characteristic of Canadian society" and committed to "...a policy of multiculturalism designed to preserve and enhance the multicultural heritage of Canadians while working to achieve the equality of all Canadians in the economic, cultural and political life of Canada[i]," implementation strategies did not include a thorough review of curriculum or institutional practices that prevented the desired levelling of the playing field. Over time, this approach was seen by many critical analysts and members of marginalized communities as mainly a celebration of food, dance and ceremonial dress styles (Mansfield and Kehoe 1993, quoted in Carrington and Bonnett, 1997, p. 415). There was and remains a failure to pursue genuine cultural equality that coincides with multicultural rhetoric.

The multicultural view does not suggest that there are deep roots to current realities. The "celebration of difference" implies that the social realities we see are the result and manifestation of a natural and preordained order. The citizenship training provided under this policy omits historical and structural information that would offer more meaningful explanations

---

i *Preamble, last para.*

for the social relationships existing in the 'Canadian mosaic', a 'mosaic' that reflects the diverse make-up of contemporary Canadian populations, but does not highlight its highly stratified layout as described in John Porter's eponymous 1965 analysis, *The Vertical Mosaic.* "Mosaic" and "Multiculturalism," favoured over the American "melting pot," emphasize the coexistence of the various cultural groups residing in this country... But public discourse generally limits the term to describing only part of the nation's citizenry in adherence to a tripartite image of a Canada consisting of the British-French majority, the aboriginal population and the "multicultural community"....While such use of "multicultural" and "cultural" may facilitate reference to certain sections of the population, it also fosters the institutionalized separation of the mainstream from "les autres" (Karim 1989, in 'Multiculturalism in Public Discourse', reprinted in (ed.) E. C. Karpinski, *Pens of Many Colours*, 1997: 141).

As well, multiculturalism as either policy or analysis did not address the formative issues of the Canadian state: colonial dispossession, Indigenous sovereignty, or the contemporary position of First Nations within Canada. Indigenous structures, including traditional authority, forms of governance, and the colonial Band Councils, were excluded from the definitions of institutions covered by the policy. There was no parallel policy to address the deprivations caused by this divorce from the Canadian state without compensatory recognition of Indigenous statehood.

Analysts have suggested that "Canada's policy of multiculturalism developed principally as a social and political measure to promote Canadian unity...a philosophy in which minority differences are accepted as an intrinsic component of the social and political order...it guarantees the right freely to pursue the cultural lifestyle of one's choice..." (Raptis and Fleming, 1998: 3)

This was patently not applicable to Indigenous peoples whose rights to cultural difference, specificity, or autonomy have been violently denied. State policy toward Indigenous peoples remains violent as the ongoing separation of the peoples from their land continues. Multiculturalism tended to create an artificial and exclusionary "us" (i.e. all who fall under and identify with the multicultural rubric) and "them" (i.e., all others)

Through the 1970s, the main benefits from multiculturalism were the recognition, validation, and support of a variety of cultural practices, heightened levels of cultural understanding that had a positive impact on life in Toronto and other major Canadian cities, and a political environment in which advocacy around difference could take root. Communities whose cultures had value within existing power structures were able to have some level of social participation, ranging from providing services or entertainment – such as food in Chinatown, or tourism around Caribana, to inclusion in policy-making on issues that affected them, and the creation and growth of NGOs advocating for a range of rights and solutions. Many advisory groups, policy bodies and community organizations had their start under multicultural programs.

Multicultural policy and programming offered no direct avenues to address issues of class, disability, or sexual identity. However, access and community development enabled during this era did a great deal to empower communities. It was lobbying by immigrant communities, by visible minority advocates, and by women and social justice activists that spurred official recognition of systemic discrimination against particular groups and subsequent social and economic costs. In 1986 the first Employment Equity Act was passed, designating four groups for prioritization in the workforce: women, Aboriginal people, visible minorities, and people with disabilities.

Areas of Contention Delineated in the Multicultural Approach

The multicultural approach[i] emphasizes:

- INTERGROUP HARMONY
- EDUCATIONAL UNDERACHIEVEMENT
- INDIVIDUAL PREJUDICE
- EQUALITY OF OPPORTUNITY
- IMPROVING SELF-IMAGE THROUGH PRIDE IN CULTURAL HERITAGE

The above, briefly reviewed, individually as follows, can be used as the basis for discussion.

INTERGROUP HARMONY

Intergroup harmony is certainly desirable, but can it be achieved without recognizing the historical privilege and marginalization on which current realities are founded? Can harmony be attained without intergroup equity called for in the anti-racist approach? (See Section Two). Harmony implies agreement, synchrony, and concord. Inequitable situations typically generate resentment, dissatisfaction, and guilt.

---

i *Mansfield, Earl; Kehoe, John 1994. "A Critical Examination of Anti-Racist Education." Canadian Journal of Education.*

EDUCATIONAL UNDERACHIEVEMENT AND SOCIAL CONTEXT

Can educational underachievement or other sociological phenomena be explained without reference to their social context? A critical analysis would include defining the role of history and consequent structures. The multicultural approach in separating social effects from their historical antecedents, sought to manage these effects with programs and guidelines such as the Heritage/International Language programs established with funding and support to "facilitate the acquisition, retention and use of all languages that contribute to the multicultural heritage of Canada." However, these languages are not granted equal status with the two 'official' settler languages. By supporting a wide range of the community without altering the fundamental power relations, the program functions to enable acceptability of the status quo across an expanded base of stakeholders[i].

Martin & Nakayama (2004, 2007) state: "Groups that have the most power (whites, men, heterosexuals) consciously or unconsciously formulate a communication system that supports their perception of the world...co-cultural group members (ethnic minorities, women, gays) must function in communication systems that often do not represent their experiences. Non-dominant groups thus find themselves in dialectical struggles: Do they try to adapt to the dominant communications style, or do they maintain their own styles? (226)....The languages we speak and the languages others think we should speak can create barriers in intercultural communication (241)...identity, language, and history create tensions between who we think we are and who others think we are (241)....Language policies are embedded in the politics of class, culture, ethnicity, and economics (242)....Sometimes nations decide on a national language as part of a process of driving people to assimilate into the national culture (242)....We can view the development of language policies as reflecting the dialectical tensions between the nation's history and its future, between the various language communities, and between economic and political relations inside and outside the nation. Language policies can help resolve or exacerbate these tensions" (244).

The government of Saskatchewan states unequivocally that "Encouraging students to take pride in their own cultures promotes respect for members of other cultures." This is a large claim which is not proven by outcomes, and which obscures the underlying role of education in "promoting the values of dominant and elite groups" (Raptis and Fleming 1998:2).

---

i *Mansfield and Kehoe (1)*

Carl James (1995) describes this role: "For the most part, minority groups and immigrants have had to change elements of their behaviour... in order to gain access to institutions....While they may maintain some aspect of their ancestral culture, by and large, their cultural practices reflect the parameters placed upon them by the laws, values, and codes of behaviour developed and institutionalized by the English and French" (35).

What is your position regarding Canada's bilingual language policy? Do you believe that such parameters are desirable, undesirable, essential, unworkable or non-essential in a multicultural society?

Another key program born out of Canada's multicultural policy is the now well-established Black/African History Month, an annual forum sponsored by boards of education in which African-Canadian communities can learn about and embrace their cultural origins, and others can educate themselves on these often obscured histories. The July 2007 "Canadian Heritage" website describes the month as "a time to celebrate the many achievements and contributions of Black Canadians, who throughout history, have done so much to make Canada the culturally diverse, compassionate and prosperous nation we know today. It is also an opportunity for the majority of Canadians to learn about the experiences of Black Canadians in our society, and the vital role this community has played throughout our shared history."[i]

What is your position on this? Do you think that "Black" Canadians have been assigned a homogenous place in society? Are Black peoples from various parts of Africa, the Caribbean, Latin America, along with the descendants from Black families who came to Canada in the 19th century homogenous? Is there an understanding of the heterogeneity of 'Black' peoples?

Typically, the multicultural approach neither recognizes nor highlights the full historical context. The "vital role" of 'Blacks' as expressed in the Saskatchewan website noted above, was as cheap labour with no rights and no protection from 'owners' or employers, many of whom prospered as a result of this labour. The often brutal context of enslavement through which many African/Black peoples became integrated into Canadian society is barely, if ever, mentioned in educational texts or media. Winks (1997) in The Blacks in Canada: A History, makes the following observation: "Indeed, most white Canadians would not have learned that there were Negroes in Canada. All had to rely on their formal schooling. Textbooks forgot that Black men existed after 1865, and only a few Canadian books gave even passing reference to the influx of fugitive slaves in the 1850s. Most did not mention Canada's own history of slavery, and none referred

---

i *http://www.pch.gc.ca/progs/multi/black-noir/index_e.cfm*

to Negroes—or to separate schools—after discussing the American Civil War" (363).

Highlighting and prioritizing these facts is essential to effectively rupturing historical exclusion in educational materials, and redressing the power imbalances evident in how history is told.

INDIVIDUAL (AND COLLECTIVE) PREJUDICE IN EDUCATION

To what extent is individual prejudice responsible for discrimination? Collective prejudice has been codified in institutions, enabling individually-held bias to become normalized, tacit, and automatic. Thus the individual is absolved of consequences following his or her actions that upon close scrutiny would reveal a discriminatory intent. The normalized Eurocentric worldview, infused within curricula in our educational institutions, provides ample opportunities to reject, castigate, insult, and scorn cultural beliefs that do not coincide with it. We have seen this in the past and must be aware that it remains active in present-day classrooms.

Marimba Ani (1994) makes the point when she says that Toynbee "has made it clear that in his view Europeans are the people responsible for 'Western civilization'. This is the kind of definition that is assumed as we make our way through the plethora of undergraduate required courses, texts, television, and even movie spectaculars that deal with 'Western civilization' Eurocentrically (19)....The most insidious expression of European nationalism is manifested in the process of codification through which behavior and thought patterns have been standardized by validating theoretical formulations provided by European academia. We need only to decode its workings in order to understand the mechanisms of supremacy and break its power." (24)

Individuals and communities that suffer under the yoke of discrimination are faced with the impervious and often inscrutable facades and practices of institutions whose 'democratic' credentials are implicit, entrenched, hegemonic, and virtually untouchable. Furthermore, institutions cannot be questioned or challenged without organized, resourced, sustainable efforts.

> [T]here are ongoing incidents of discrimination in our society that require our continuing attention. In fact, the Supreme Court of Canada in 2005 acknowledged that racial prejudice against visible minorities is so notorious and indisputable that its existence needs to be treated as a social fact. (*R. v. Spence*, [2005] 3 S.C.R. 458, para. 5), quoted in Ontario's Equity and Inclusive Education Strategy (2009: 7)

EQUALITY OF OPPORTUNITY

Equality of opportunity is an obvious social good and the answer to many of the grievances around discrimination or monoculturalism. Providing a wider more accurate flow of information with more access points would allow more people from diverse backgrounds to take advantage of increased opportunities, as has yet to be the case in the educational system at *all levels*. However, within society in general, more opportunities have not in themselves transformed the life outcomes of all populations equally or equitably. Just as affirmative action programs have historically been shown to benefit the White male most, equity programs have given more to those who already had advantages. Thus, *equality of outcome* is a different goal, one that would allow disadvantaged communities and individuals to not only knock on the door of opportunity, but be welcomed across the threshold. Access in Canada is immediately witnessed in many job advertisements wherein employers often state they are *equal opportunity* employers. Without exhausting the semantics, we can readily understand that e*qual opportunity access* does not automatically mean *equal opportunity outcome*, and therein lies the root of the problem.

The outcry against corrective programming that benefited some communities of colour was often based on the perception that 'other' people (White immigrants) had not been helped or given special services or grants. Overlooked is the one prevailing factor that differentiated White immigrants from Blacks – whiteness. As Dionne Brand has noted, whiteness "was like money and still is.[i]"

PRIDE IN CULTURAL HERITAGE

Programs to promote cultural retention and celebration are advocated in both the multicultural and anti-racist approaches, and are key strategies for equipping disadvantaged communities and individuals to grow their self-knowledge, and for dominant groups to have their embedded assumptions and entitlements challenged. The point of difference is in whether they are seen as ends in themselves (as in multiculturalism) or as stages in a much more profound social change. Additionally, these programs benefit White, European communities with their much greater 'racial capital' as much as they do communities of colour, raising the issue of *equity vs. equality.*

---

i *Brand, Dionne, "Notes for Writing Through Race," p. 175. In Bread out of a Stone, Coach House Press, Toronto 1995.*

The first step...toward an antiracist education is to become aware of white   privilege and normativity and disrupt the cycle.

(Volgyi, 2006: 10)

ANTI-RACISM

Anti-racism work began as a response to the perceived limitations of multiculturalism to modify the structural inadequacies that affected the access and servicing of growing numbers of individuals and their communities. The main problem areas included existing immigrant and integration services, along with lack of appropriate settlement programs and ongoing social support. Many persons experienced problematized access to education and training opportunities. Multiculturalism did not address barriers that systematically excluded particular populations and communities –such as language and credential requirements that privileged the Anglo-Francophone settler cultures. These barriers, sustained throughout the educational, service, and employment sectors, served to maintain the hierarchy of White upper- and upper-middle power-holders, with citizens of colour massed along the bottom of the social triangle. A few faces of colour scattered through the upper layers were used as an argument against challenges to the overall system.

In 1985, the provincial government issued an *Ontario Policy on Race Relations*, committing itself to "an active role in the elimination of all racial discrimination..." But existing social dynamics were too antagonistic for superficial measures to have serious effect. These dynamics, evident in all too many instances throughout society, affect our schools and workplaces today, making it particularly crucial that teachers create classroom environments wherein equity and respect are clear and practiced. Case (2002) states: "If we consider the extent of our responsibilities as teachers, can we ever permit ourselves at any stage to prejudge the capacities, the motivation, the effort of a pupil without determining the education of that pupil in such a way that our prophecy is fulfilled? If we prejudge entire groups of people, the poor, Asians, Italians, Koreans, then we relegate them to one distorted position within our society. We must never underestimate the extent of our responsibility or the extent of harm that we can cause." (54-55)

Prejudgment and harm have a historical basis in Canadian education. With regard to First Nations peoples, Frideres & Gadacz note that between 1867 and 1945, "Scant attention was paid to developing a curriculum geared to either their language difficulties or

27

their sociological needs....Provincial governments were too preoccupied with their own priorities to become involved in Indian [sic] education. Missionaries provided a modicum of services, but their 'noble savage' philosophy effectively insulated the Indians [sic] from the mainstream of society" (Special Hearing on Poverty, 1970: 14, 59, as referenced by Frideres & Gadacz, 7th ed. 2005: 109). They go on to state: "Because they felt that Aboriginal people would always live in isolation, the missionaries made no attempt to prepare them for successful careers in modern Canadian society. Instead, they concentrated on eradicating all traces of Aboriginal languages, traditions, and beliefs." (Fuchs, 1970, as referenced by Frideres & Gadacz, (109)

Anti-racism analysis, in addressing such issues from both historical and contemporary standpoints, offers information and understanding about how entrenched discrimination and consequent marginalization of 'others' came to be normalized. Several very real factors and events must be acknowledged: the Canadian state's origins as a colonizing force that had invaded lands inhabited for several millennia by Indigenous peoples; the ever encroaching settlements of territories through force and coercion; the introduction of Black people relegated to little more than slaves and menials; the use of underpaid and abused Chinese labour to build icons of modern Canadian development such as the trans-Canada railroad; the longstanding use of farm workers from the Caribbean as 'guest workers'; the ongoing exploitation of women from the Philippines and the Caribbean to act as nannies for upper-class households; the ways in which media representation influenced and influences social perceptions; and government policies that served to maintain inequity. These histories and other relevant information are essential for a genuine comprehension of the current realities affecting the entire educational system from Grade 1 through post-secondary levels.

The most recent (2009) report, *Ontario's Equity and Inclusive Education Strategy*, states, "We believe that Ontario's diversity can be one of its greatest assets. To realize the promise of diversity, we must ensure that we respect and value the full range of our differences. Equitable, inclusive education is also central to creating a cohesive society and a strong economy that will secure Ontario's future prosperity (5). ...To date only forty-three of Ontario's seventy-two school boards report that they currently have some form of equity policy in place. These policies range from a one-page statement to comprehensive documents accompanied by guidelines and resource materials." (9)

An anti-racism approach is salient toward advancing the equity and inclusive education mentioned in the report.

Areas of Contention Delineated in the Anti-Racism Approach

Anti-racism emphasizes[i]:

INTERGROUP EQUITY

ECONOMIC DISADVANTAGE

INSTITUTIONAL RACISM

EQUALITY OF OUTCOME

UNEQUAL POWER RELATIONSHIPS

INTERGROUP EQUITY

Anti-racist training examines power imbalances as key contributors to discriminatory behaviour.

Discussion Point

- What would render interactions between unequal players positive, equitable, and beneficial for both parties?

ECONOMIC DISADVANTAGE

As noted in Ontario's 2009 Inclusive Education Strategy, "Education directly influences students' life chances – and life outcomes. Today's global, knowledge-based economy makes the ongoing work in our schools critical to our students' success in life and to Ontario's economic future. As an agent of change and social cohesion, our education system *supports and reflects* (italics the authors') the democratic values of fairness, equity, and respect for all. The schools we create today will shape the society that we and our children share tomorrow." (6)

This is laudable, except that the very need for an "inclusive education strategy" is, ipso facto, evidence that our education system does not currently support and reflect the democratic values of fairness, equity, and respect for all, hence the need for an anti-racist approach within the education system.

Discussion Points

- Who has control of resources in our environments?
- Who benefits from existing structures?
- What is each community's relationship with the main societal structures?
- What can teachers do to advance the goals of fairness, equity and respect?

---

i *Mansfield and Kehoe (1)*

INSTITUTIONAL RACISM

Institutional racism is a form of racism which is structured into political and social institutions. It occurs when institutions, including corporations, governments and universities, discriminate either deliberately or indirectly against certain groups of people to limit their rights. It reflects the cultural assumptions of the dominant group, so that the practices of that group are seen as the norm to which other cultural practices should conform (Anderson and Taylor (2006)[i].

This type of racism is distinguishable from *individual* bigotry or racial bias in that it reflects the normalized systemic behaviour of institutions or corporations whose actions indicate a pattern of discrimination based on race and ethnicity, leading to structural exclusionary practices.

Typically, such exclusion, for example, is witnessed in the height and weight requirements for police and firefighters, based on Western European 'norms', and with no regard for persons from other cultural groups where these 'stature' requirements are inconsistent with the physical realities of that particular group.

Discussion Points

- What effect would systemic racism have on your access to an institution, bureaucracy, or corporation?
- How can structural exclusionary practices be challenged for a positive outcome?
- What ideas or suggestions do you have regarding inclusion of specific materials in educational texts?

"In order for us to create an inclusive curriculum, there is a need for a total curriculum transformation where critical issues of diversity are integrated into all aspects of educational programs." (Wane, 2007: 16)

"In the educational system the curriculum materials are central. For transformative learning it is essential the materials and readings...go beyond token information provided about different cultures usually found at the back of the text, for these only serve as platitudes towards so-called 'special interest groups' and do not address the real problem of inequity experienced among subordinate people." (Wane, 2007: 16)

---

i *http://institutonalracism. net/default.aspx (accessed 4/25/2009)*

CULTIVATING POLITICAL AGENCY THROUGH CRITICAL ANALYSIS

The anti-racist approach involves an examination of racism within historical contexts, then utilizing strategies for analyzing the 'actors' and actions within historical and contemporary milieus. Workshop training attempts to motivate participants toward an understanding of their roles in changing existing systemic exclusionary practices and policies as well as their own social behaviours and choices.

Transforming consciousness demands an in-depth grasp of discriminatory behaviours in society, their causes and their remedies. At its core, anti-racism examines how European hegemony rationalized colonizing far-flung lands as an attempt to bring 'civilization' to Indigenous peoples, while at the same time promoting an inherent superiority of 'Whiteness' and European culture, achieved through its establishment of political systems, attendant religions, and 'superior' socio-cultural 'norms'.

Historically, North America's settler colonists crossed the ocean as commercial entrepreneurs and religious seekers of 'freedom' in the New World. Fishing and the fur trade initially necessitated reliance on Native peoples, but very quickly evolved into social, economic, and military dominance over invaded Indigenous territories. Settler worldviews, fueled by a belief in a religious 'ordination' by God to bring 'light' to the 'savages', saw missionaries imposing their catechisms and practices on Native peoples. Eventually these practices, over time, would evolve into total control of Indigenous populations. Beck, Walters, and Francisco (1977) state: "Educational and other assimilation policies on the part of government agencies were designed to change or destroy the sacred teachings and practices of *The People*. And...missionaries from different Christian denominations played a major role in carrying out this task." (151)

The imposition of European civilization norms became a *fait accompli*.

In Canada, as industrial enterprises expanded under the Canadian state, policy, legislation, and customary practice developed to further extend the privilege of dominant groups composed of White men. The Anglophone ruling classes won the settler power struggle, establishing dominance over their Francophone partners in the colonization thrust. Between them they established a power-sharing agreement that completely excluded the Indigenous occupants of the land mass they renamed Canada, and developed a set of norms and practices that reified their military superiority and its concomitant privileges.

Governing was based on protecting that power, and ensuring their economic control and benefit (Miller, 1989; Robinson and Quinney, 1985). In addition, as the decades passed, immigration policies would enshrine these benefits, attaching them to white-skinned immigrants. A review of modern immigration policies and structures shows the economic and labour-force motivations for all immigration that gave entry to people of colour. Increased populations of colour and of non-English speaking Whites in no way modified the English and French settler communities' "central role in defining Canadian society and culture." (James, 1995: 16)

In a nutshell, similar hegemonic practices were played out against not only Black immigrant groups, but also those who came to Canada from far flung lands such as South Asians from Vietnam, Laos, and Cambodia.

Much more can be said or written about the contexts from which immigrants to Canada originated and originate. The policies around immigration of other groups (the Chinese as one example) provide an insight into the historical fabric that underpinned historical Canadian settlement.

Discussion Points

- What difference does this kind of information make regarding your analysis of the realities of today's Canadian "mosaic?"

- What are your views regarding Indigenous people and their place in Canadian society?

- What are your thoughts regarding Blacks in Canada? Are your feelings or thoughts based on stereotypes?

- What do you know about Asians beyond their cuisines?

- What do you know about the histories of your colleagues, friends, fellow students and workers from the countries that supply most of North America's raw materials that underpin its wealth? Are you interested in knowing more about other cultures beside their dances and traditional foods?

> The recognition that Western society is fundamentally structured along the relations and dynamics of difference, coupled with the awareness that these structures and practices are contrary to a just and equitable society, has not concurrently moved us from the idea of an anti-racist, antisexist society to the application of the necessary changes in institutional practices, social processes and relations.
>
> Calliste and Dei, 2000: 13

INTEGRATIVE ANTI-RACISM

In reviewing fundamental and earlier anti-racist paradigms, analysts would conclude that established anti-racist approaches were too limited in scope. George Dei's examination of the state of 'race knowledge' posited the "myriad forms of racism, based not only on perceived phenotypical differences between peoples, but also on a conflation of religious, cultural, class, language, gender and sexual difference among people" (Dei 1995: 12). Proposing a more inclusive set of questions which situated the anti-racist analysis as one component of an individual's lived experience rather than the only or primary focus, led to the development of the 'integrative anti-racism' approach. This analysis clarified the reality that "individuals are socialized into identities corresponding to our shared and contested meanings of race, gender, class and sexuality." (Calliste and Dei, 2000: 11)

In her pioneering 'Anti-Racist Lens' concept, Enid Lee similarly identified some of these issues: "I can see how the ways in which we have organized our lives and our institutions around race and other identities have brought us to our present positions. These and other identities include language, nationality, immigration status, culture and faith, which are often racialized.[i]"

Anti-racist scholars have identified a need for educators "to reflect upon the ways in which normative (societal and educational) discourses influence their own classroom practices as well as interrogate how their culture, race, class, gender, and sexuality identities are implicated in our ways of knowing and indeed, of knowledge itself." (Wane 2007: 16)

---

i *Enid Lee website http://www.enidlee.com/ (accessed April 2007)*

GENDER

As Angela Davis discussed in her seminal work, *Women, Race and Class* (1983), many antislavery campaigners "failed to integrate their anti-slavery consciousness into their analysis of women's oppression." (66) Similarly, many feminists then and later failed to develop a class and race analysis, and these omissions prevented the movements from identifying their commonalities. More contemporary feminist analyses further refined these observations.

In their 1998 article, Fellows and Razack state: "Systems of oppression (capitalism, imperialism and patriarchy) rely on one another in complex ways. This "interlocking" effect means that the systems of oppression come into existence in and through one another so that class exploitation could not be accompanied without gender and racial hierarchies; imperialism could not function without class exploitation, sexism, heterosexism and so on." (335) Under patriarchy, gender oppression is "classified"; women are identified as "second-class" citizens, as a lower class of being, and are disempowered as a gender within and across their class status.

CLASS

When we talk about class in society, we engage differing concepts in our conception of class structure. We must determine whether we are talking analytically or empirically. Analytically, we would generally theorize that class denotes hierarchical stratifications between societal groups or cultures. Empirically, we would conceptualize class as being based on any number of practical indicators – wealth, education, family origins, job, etc. However, although age, race, religion, gender or sexual orientation lack hierarchal implications, they are not normally considered under the heading of social class. But if we examine this further, we can arguably conclude that the stratification between *dominant* races and ethnic groups in Canada and the United States point to both analytical *and* empirical class distinctions *regardless* of age, gender, colour, race, wealth, education, or sexual orientation.

In racialized societies, race and colour often become interchangeable with class categories; under White supremacy, people of colour are subject to the domination of white cultural normativeness regardless of class – a person of colour is acceptable to White people insofar as "that person thinks and acts like them, shares their values and beliefs, is in no way different..." (hooks 1995: 185)

Skin colour privilege creates class characteristics, access, material opportunities, social position, economic advantage and mobility. Yet, at the same time, economic success by a person of colour can clearly still provide some refuge from blatant racism through the ability to live in certain areas, purchase certain comforts, and navigate hierarchies with greater ease. Despite this, there is always the reality of the prevailing socio-racial contexts that are based on entrenched assumptions of racial superiority.

However, and importantly, it must be recognized that class stratification and conflict are not necessarily or *solely* based on colour. As Case (2002) points out: "The major division that exists among Blacks in Canada appears to be that of class and not of geographic origin....Middle class Blacks of Canadian, Caribbean and African origins mistrust one another deeply even though occasional crises force them to unite in the interest of preserving their class privileges. What is unfortunate is that their struggles for recognition, acceptance and assimilation often result in the fostering of conflict between working class Blacks of Canadian, African and Caribbean origins." (105, 106)

And although we witness class stratification within White communities, we know from empirical evidence that in many regions of North America, a White person of little education or wealth is accepted by the dominant culture as 'superior' to a Black person of education and wealth *simply because* he or she is White.

Thus emerges a further layer of complexity when we consider the subject of class: race and colour are not the only restrictors or sites of contestation, even though it is all too often *the* crucial barrier to upward mobility and significant economic attainment by so-called minorities within existing institutional structures.

Discussion Points

- What is your definition of class?
- What role do cultural practices play in forming class distinctions?
- What is your reaction to Case's (2002) description of Black class conflict?
- Are there similarities between Black class conflict and race/ethnic conflict?

SEXUAL ORIENTATION

Many current analyses have identified issues of homophobia and fear of sexuality as extensions of the misogyny associated with patriarchy. Homosexual men, lesbians, and transsexual people face discrimination, threats, assaults and insults, and deprivation of their rights just as do many racialized persons. And when these individuals are both homosexual and racialized, they are subject to 'double' discrimination, with many shunned within their communities of origin, communities that may have conservative views on sexual orientation. Many progressive activist groups whose advocacy on race issues is strong and committed, are not responsive to the LGBT community's political positions and needs.

> The terrors homosexuals go through in this society would not be so great if the society itself did not go through so many terrors which it doesn't want to admit. The discovery of one's sexual preference doesn't have to be a trauma. It's a trauma because it's such a traumatized society.
>
> James Baldwin in a 1984 interview conducted by Richard Goldstein. in (ed.) Quincy Troupe. *James Baldwin: The Legacy* (1989:

In 1986, sexual orientation was added to the Ontario Human Rights Code, and the issues began to be more widely acknowledged as impacting significant numbers of people, having educational, social, and political implications. Recognition from the mid-1990s onward of the intersection of identities and subsequent impact on life experiences has enabled a multitude of analyses to surface. These have presented many challenges to feminism and anti-racism as noted in a review of a collection of critical pieces by Krista Scott-Dixon in Trans/Forming Feminisms: Transfeminist Voices Speak Out. She makes the point that while gender analysis lies at feminism's foundation, complex intersections of trans-sexuality are often omitted categorically from feminism, which has seldom welcomed the participation of "trans-activists and thinkers." The Toronto Trans and Two-Spirit Primer, prepared at 519 Church Community Centre, notes: "It is often the intersection of racism, classism, ableism, ageism, and other forms of linking oppressions that create the barriers that the lower-income trans community faces."

Discussion Points

- Do you think, as Baldwin (above) stated, that society reacts to homosexuals the way it does because it is going through its own trauma?

- What are your own feelings regarding homosexuality?

- How would you respond to someone who voiced anti-homosexual, anti-lesbian sentiments? Would you respond at all?

CULTURE AND RELIGIOUS FAITH

There is no question that the Western world subscribes to Christianity and Catholicism as major cultural-religious pillars. Adherents of both religions were culpable in both the trade in human beings from Africa and the subjugation of Indigenous peoples across the Americas during the European conquest of the New World. Christianity as practiced in Anglophone Canada, and Catholicism as practiced in Francophone Quebec, were formative in the development of their respective social, political, economic, and educational foundations. To observe this fact of history is not to criticize this reality. However, and importantly, institutionalized rituals attached to both beliefs are considered sacrosanct, and from a *national* standpoint, rituals and religious practices of peoples who are neither Christian nor Catholic are essentially marginalized. The complexity, as with so much of Canada's endeavours, is multi-faceted: rituals and holidays that are Jewish, or Muslim, or Hindu, are accepted as part of Canada's multiculturalism policy, but do not form part of official state religious practices.

From the standpoint of Blacks, not only in Canada but across the Western World, the impact of Christianity is immediately evidenced in the surnames Blacks carry; these names are not African, but European; their first languages are English, French, or Spanish. Their holiday observances derive from Christianity or Eurocentric paganism (Easter bunny, Easter eggs, Santa Claus, Halloween, Christmas). For Africans of the Diaspora, one specific and growing development has been the observance of Kwanzaa, celebrated during the 'Christmas' season. Since its inception in 1966 by Dr. Maulana "Ron" Karenga, this celebration has never been not religious, but cultural, a "time for African-Americans to reflect upon their rich cultural heritage as products of two worlds" (McClester, 1990, 1985, *Kwanzaa*, p. iii). The series of rituals spread over seven days (begun after Christmas) pay tribute to the cultural roots of Americans of African ancestry, and over the past 40 years since inception, have been adopted by increasing numbers of Black non-Americans in Canada and the Caribbean.

However, and specifically with regard to culture and religious faith of Blacks in Canada, the majority are practitioners of the Christian faith, and subscribe to the cultural mores that such a belief encompasses. Yet, despite this belief, for many during the Christmas season there is a celebration of both Christmas and Kwanzaa, constituting a symbiosis of Euro-centered and African-centered religious and cultural practice.

Also, no Indigenous days or ceremonies are recognized at either the provincial or federal level, and the Chinese New Year, Eid, and Ramadan are generally restricted to the relevant communities.

SPOKEN LANGUAGE

The variety of accents, dialects, vernaculars, and colloquialisms in English language usage seem as numerous as the countries colonized and cultures displaced by Anglo and American imperialism. Even in England, the home of the English language, there are regional vernaculars and dialects. Similarly in the United States, where English is the official language, there are accents and colloquialisms peculiar to specific regions. However, while in England and America the English language reflects a *natural* cultural development, for peoples whose lands (in Africa and the Americas) have been colonized, English is a cultural imposition). "Every colonized people—in other words, every people in whose soul an inferiority complex has been created by the death and burial of its local cultural originality—finds itself face to face with the language of the civilizing nation; that is, with the culture of the mother country" (Fanon, 1967: 18).

This is readily evident with the Indigenous peoples of North America, whose history of being forcibly denied speaking their native cultural languages is generally known. "[C]hildren were sent to boarding schools where they were not allowed to speak their own language....In terms of the cultural attitudes examined, these schools, like the words used to name *The People*, were designed to break the spirit of *The People*" (Beck et al. (1997: 150). To reorient peoples through the use of language served as a crucial vehicle by which to impose a social structure acceptable to the colonizing power. "A language is a connected set of speech usages observed within a defined speech-community. The existence of speech-communities and their sizes are features of social structure. There is, therefore, a certain very general relation between social structure and language." (Radcliffe-Brown (1987: 128).

Language, constituting a major tool of cultural imperialism, has had a fundamental effect on the nature of relations between peoples. One of the defining characteristics of the language-based social dynamic is that command of not only the grammar but also the accent of native-speaker English usage, is a hidden but powerful signifier of the roles that people will play or be allowed to play in Canadian society. Those who sound like native speakers are at the top of this hierarchy, and those who speak with accents that deviate from *acceptable* English are often subject to negative assumptions about their intellectual capacities and educational levels. Language is an important but little discussed aspect of stereotyping. However, if the presence of an accent clearly denotes that the mother tongue is not English, but another European language—best of all, French—then it can actually become an asset. Multilingual *European* language skills are seen as an important socio-cultural indication of learning capacity and are a valuable commodity in the Canadian marketplace. The ability to speak one or more First Nations languages is not considered an asset.

DISABILITY

Between 2001 and 2006 the persons who reported having a disability in Canada increased by three-quarters of a million (+21.2%), reaching 4.4 million in 2006[i]. When one speaks of persons with a disability, we recognize that disability is a mental, sensory, or emotional impairment that interferes with the major tasks of daily living. (48)[ii] All too often those with disabilities are marginalized. "Discriminatory practices continue to deny persons with disabilities, as well as workers who become disabled, access to work. Two-thirds of the unemployed respondents with disabilities said they would like to work but could not find jobs."

People with disabilities experience closed doors and barriers to participation in our institutions – school, social services, and businesses – often on grounds that are stereotypical with no true relation to their capacity to work and contribute to the larger community. In Toronto schools, the issues raised by disability were initially addressed by Special

---

i *http://www.disabled-world.com/disability/statistics/disability-statistics-canada_printer.php (accessed 5/1/2009)*

ii *Locker/Findlay, McGraw-Hill Ryerson, Business Communication Now, Canadian Edition (2009)*

Education programs that did provide services enabling access to the educational system, but these were largely in segregated environments and in practice perpetuated many of the societal problems experienced by community of people with disabilities, or disabled people. By the late 1990s, a very effective lobby had grown and was able to participate in the discussions and actions that sought to bring about reform in Ontario legislation and institutions. This campaign has also experienced many of the same difficulties as with the anti-racism struggles: one set of barriers is toppled; a new set of barriers is created.

Discussion Points

- Do you believe, as do some employers, that physically disabled persons are incapable of being effective in the workplace?

- What have been your own interactions with disabled persons?

- Do you see similarities between the barriers disabled persons face and those faced by marginalized peoples?

- What paths can we take to realize our common oppressions (gender, race, ethnicity), barriers, and means of resistance?

DECOLONIZING ANTI-RACISM

Bonita Lawrence and Enakshi Dua[i] present cogent arguments about the inadequacies of established anti-racism approaches for understanding or incorporating Indigenous people's histories and current realities in Canada. Since Canada is situated in the same space at the same time, there is an unavoidable need to arrive at a position on Indigenous rights, and to prioritize this analysis within any anti-racism discussion and practice. Yet, such discussion and prioritizing are absent in much anti-racism training.

Lawrence and Dua present a series of analytical points that can help us develop a more comprehensive critique of colonization in the North American context. They begin their deconstruction with two guiding questions: *What does it mean to look at Canada as a colonized space? What does it mean to ignore Indigenous sovereignty?*

When we view Canadian history through the decolonizing lens, we witness many facts that have been obscured in State education. The pre-European landmass is presented as a landscape needing to be tamed by hardy, ingenious, divinely-ordained pioneers. With zeal, the colonizers began to shape the land and the Native peoples they found in

i *Bonita Lawrence and Enakshi Dua, Decolonising AntiRacism (2005).*

their own image of what constituted 'civilization' and progress. "Clashes between European powers and the indigenous peoples of the Americas began almost immediately upon the arrival of the first Europeans on the shores of the New World....The great disparity between the two cultures, particularly their differing concepts of land ownership, made peaceful coexistence virtually impossible." (Keenan (1999: ix)

In 2007, Dr. Dawn Martin Hill[i] gave an estimate of 17 million Indigenous people killed in the first 200 years of land appropriation by Canada and its preceding entities –traders, the early corporations, and the early forms of colonial government. She is being conservative; some recent investigations cite evidence for figures between 50 million and 100 million.

Whole populations were wiped out, and the story of those exterminations is one marked by extreme brutality and sadism[ii]. This is but one of the many historical facts omitted from standard school and university textbooks and official materials on Canadian history (See Appendix "A").

Another aspect that the decolonizing lens can illuminate for us are the "ideological vehicles" used by Dr. Hill to construct and disseminate the images that promote an ideology. Whatever the numbers of Native peoples killed, those bodies did exist, did act, and have been omitted from the landscapes of our knowledge and consciousness. History has been sanitized by European hegemony. That many First Nations peoples view the destruction of bodies, the systematic decimation of Aboriginal cultures, the forced separation of First Nations children from their families, and the relentless assault on Aboriginal languages as "genocide" should not be surprising.

In a column[iii] titled 'Toronto's diversity not as perfect as we think', Royson James noted in regard to an Aboriginal woman's comment: "she still chafes at the reality of residential schools. She grieved for thousands still unaccounted for; kids forcibly removed from kin, and

---

i *The talk, 'Out of the Shadows: Deconstructing the Colonial Woman', was given 22 May 2007, at Catalyst Café, Native Canadian Centre, Toronto, by Dr. Dawn Martin-Hill (Mohawk, Wolf Clan) from Six Nations; Academic Director of the Indigenous Studies Program at McMaster University.*

ii *Such as the Beothuk in the "new found land" that became "home" to the Canadian. In 1613, the Beothuk defend themselves against the French. The French arm the Micmac and offer bounties for Beothuk scalps, which results in the extermination of the Beothuk. (Donna Hightower-Langston, The Native American World, 2003: 44).*

iii *From the Toronto Star, Section G2, Thursday, 12 March 2009. James reports on interviews held with attendees at the one-day conference of the National Council of Visible Minorities in the federal public service.*

culturally assaulted for having their hair cropped – something not done in native culture except as a sign of intense grief or protest....And she used "genocide" to describe what has happened to the first nations of this country."

There is little doubt that many may find the use of the term "genocide" an inaccurate and perhaps inflammatory reference or reaction to historical fact. But how else can one view the *systematic* and *institutional* determination to eradicate First Nations peoples, family structures, language, spiritual practices, kidnapping of their children, and assumption of control of lands upon which the Aboriginal peoples depended for their traditional livelihoods for countless generations spanning thousands of years, not to mention (as previously noted) the physical destruction of entire tribes decimated by brutal wars as anything *but* genocide? Certainly the victims and many of their descendants across Canada and America view it as such. And another fact that illustrates genocide is noted by Hightower-Langston (2003): In 1623, "The English-Powhatan Peace Conference occurs, where the English serve glasses of poisoned wine to toast eternal friendship with the Indians. Survivors of the poisoning are shot to death." (44)

The anti-racist community participates in this denial by accepting the tacit line that the genocide has been completed and that Indigenous people therefore "no longer need to be taken into account" (Lawrence and Dua, 2005: 3). They find that "antiracism theory participates in the colonial agenda in two ways. First, it ignores the ongoing colonization of Aboriginal peoples in the Americas; second, it fails to integrate an understanding of Canada as a colonialist state into antiracism frameworks" (2). Thus the first step in expanding our antiracism analyses is an awareness of the present reality of the original peoples of Turtle Island (the name by which North American Aboriginal peoples refer to the North American continent).

Discussion Points

- What are your feelings about the term genocide?
- Do you think that denialism is an example of European hegemony and privilege?

Some Facts

The 2006 Canadian census reveals that there are more than 1.2 million Aboriginal people in Canada, which includes First Nations, Métis, and Innuit. They represent 3.8% of the total population. Compared to the expanding populations of other racialized groups, the struggle of Indigenous populations to maintain their numbers under continuing colonialism is noticeable.

According to a 2004 *Corrections and Conditional Release Statistical Overview*, Corrections Canada, the agency that oversees the federal prison system, routinely discriminates against Aboriginal offenders. Although the overall federal prison population declined by 12.5% from 1996 to 2004, the number of First Nations people in federal institutions increased by 21.7 %, and the number of incarcerated First Nations[ii] women increased by a staggering 74.2% over the same period. In addition, higher numbers of Blacks in Canada are incarcerated than Whites.

Initial reaction might be to conclude that these extraordinarily high rates of incarceration reflect a simple fact: *Black and Aboriginal peoples commit more crimes than other groups.* But such beliefs are false.

In his Paper, 'The Role of the Judiciary in Racial Profiling: A Case Study of Canada', presented at the 17th International Conference of the International Society for the Reform of Criminal Law: <u>Convergence of Criminal Justice Systems: Building Bridges – Bridging the Gaps</u>, between 24th – 28th August 2003, in the Hague[iii], The Netherlands, barrister and solicitor Munyonzwe Hamalengwa of Mississauga, Ontario, notes: "A certain conspiracy of silence is binding the entire Canadian criminal, civil and immigration systems of justice. A conspiracy of silence prevails when it comes to dealing with issues involving systemic racism and racial discrimination in Canada's criminal, civil and immigration courts and tribunals" (2). Hamalengwa makes several points in his study that document "this conspiracy of silence":

- Black males were significantly more likely than Whites or Chinese to be stopped by police.
- Blacks were less likely to receive police bail or judicial interim release than Whites. Further, a person who was not given bail was more likely to be convicted and sent to jail than a person who was on bail.
- Prosecutors were more likely to proceed to indictment when they tried a Black defendant than when they tried a White defendant.

---

i *Corrections and Conditional Release Statistical Overview released in December 2004.*

ii *From Native Women's Association of Canada release on 16 October 2006, titled: Number of Aboriginal People in Canada's Prisons Growing. www.afn.ca/cmslib/general/NAOs.pdf. (Accessed 1 May 2009).*

iii *Full report at www.isrl.ora/Papers/Davies.pdf (accessed 2 May 2009)*

Hamalengwa takes his facts from the <u>Report of the Commission on Systemic Racism in the Ontario Criminal Justice System</u>, and further to this specific report, states that it has "Documented that discrimination against blacks is usually found in systemic form and concealed in system, practices, policies and laws that may appear neutral on their face but have a serious detrimental effect on people of colour. Immigration laws, policies and practices have been informed fundamentally by racial overtones and under-tones." (4)

There is much more that Hamalengwa's study reveals about systemic and institutionalized racism in society. "The culture of racism has also been documented as pervasive in the media. A study by Ryerson Polytechnic University Professor, Frances Henry entitled, <u>The Racialization of Crime in Toronto's Print Media</u> (1999) documents how Blacks in general are criminalized in the media, particularly Black Jamaicans." (6)

Finally, with racism ever present regarding Blacks brought before Canada's judicial systems, Hamalengwa notes that, "It was no secret that white juries routinely convicted Black defendants even on flimsy evidence or acquitted White defendants even when evidence for conviction was overwhelming." (12)

Aboriginal women face similar quandaries when brought before Canada's justice systems. The Native Women's Association of Canada, in their Issue Paper, Aboriginal Women and the Legal Justice System in Canada, prepared for the National Aboriginal Women's Summit, 20-22 June, 2007, states that "One consequence of severe socio-economic marginalization resulted in Aboriginal women being over represented in the criminal justice system both as offenders and as victims of crimes. There is a strong need to address the root causes of the disproportionate incarceration rates of Aboriginal women and the high rates of criminal victimization both with the Aboriginal community and Canadian society, as evidenced by the alarmingly high rates of Aboriginal women who are missing and/or murdered." (1)

The Issue Paper also notes that "For Aboriginal women, the rates of incarceration are particularly disturbing. Correctional Service (CSC) data reveals although Aboriginal women account for only 3% of the female population in Canada, they made up 29% of the women in federal correctional facilities on July 27, 2003. Aboriginal women are not only disproportionately over represented but also the fastest growing population sentenced to federal prisons." (2)

Added to this, Aboriginal women, once incarcerated, often experience discrimination within the prisons from other inmates *and* correctional staff. The plight of these women is unconscionable in a society that vaunts itself as a democratic beacon of diversity, multiculturalism, laws, and fair play. And the abuse of power by members of the criminal justice system is glaringly evident in one particular case described in the Issue Paper thusly: "A former provincial court judge, David William Ramsey abused his power with young Aboriginal women between the ages of 12 and 16 who appeared before him in court. He had access to their personal backgrounds and psychiatric histories and promised lighter sentences if they didn't tell anyone that they were coerced to perform sexual acts for him, acts which often turned violent. He was charged with and pleaded guilty to one count of sexual assault causing bodily harm, three counts of purchasing sex from three women under the age of 18, and one count of breach of trust. It's interesting to note that he was never charged with a hate crime even though his victims were chosen based on their Aboriginal identity." (3, 4)

These facts and their implications for the whole of society are rarely discussed, much less central to anti-racism analyses and training practices. Such information is not hard to uncover, but the will to seek it and to act responsibly on our knowledge is the link we have to cultivate in ourselves and in those whose minds we are influencing through teaching, writing, and polemical guidance in all our roles as educators.

With Indigenous students and Black students sharing the highest dropout rates and the lowest rates of university applications, it is essential to recognize that, as Dei, Mazzuca, McIsaac, and Zine (1997) state "the issues of race, ethnicity, class, gender, and sexuality present significant challenges and lessons for Euro-Canadian/American schools....Many educators and educational researchers are boldly articulating the necessity and importance of understanding how youth from diverse racial, ethnic, class, and gender backgrounds are responding to the institutionalized processes and structures of schooling in Euro-American contexts....In order for schools to carry out any exemplary educational practices to establish a genuine inclusion of all students, it is crucial that there is an initial comprehension of the nature and context of the specific problems and experiences that lead some students to leave school prematurely." (3, 4)

> There is no simple cause-effect relation which characterizes Black students' disengagement from school. Dropping out is the final act of a series of school and out-of-school developments/experiences that define the student's ability to engage and disengage in a school's culture. Students drop out of school when it appears, in their view, there is no other appropriate recourse or action to take.
> Dei et al. (1997: 62-63)

Obviously, Black and Indigenous students are not typified by homogeneity. However, they are victimized, more often than not, by similar and entrenched socio-economic disadvantages, discrimination, marginalization, stereotypical views, justice-system inequities, and pre-conceived notions of their abilities and intelligence.

DECOLONIZING OUR ANALYSES

In her essay 'Overcoming White Supremacy', bell hooks writes, "It is our collective responsibility as people of color and as white people who are committed to ending white supremacy to help one another. It is our collective responsibility to educate for critical consciousness." (1995: 194)

It may be said that what hooks is referring to is the need for *intellectual decolonization*, the freeing of ourselves from the boundaries inculcated through Western hegemony. "The legacy of 500 years of Western expansion, including 200 years of Western hegemony, reflected in racism and exotism, continues to be recycled in Western cultures in the form of stereotypical images of 'non-Western' cultures." (Pieterse & Parekh (eds.), *The Decolonization of Imagination*, 1995: 4)

Rupturing this process calls for *internal* decolonization, whereby we examine the cultural politics and Eurocentric ideologies that dominate our lives and imaginations as the 'gold standard' of being and living.

> [D]ecolonization comes to be understood as an act of exorcism for both the colonizer and the colonized. For both parties it must be a process of liberation: from dependency, in the case of the decolonized, and from imperialist, racist perceptions, representations, and institutions...in the case of the colonizer.
> Mehrez, 1991: 258, as quoted in Pieterse & Parekh (eds.), (1995: 4)

How can we as educators create alliances with one other and take up the responsibility to effect "liberation" in our personal practices and in our classrooms?

We can begin by examining our intellectual and social assumptions and the environments in which we participate. In the spirit of truth-seeking, we can be free to generate our own questions for penetrating the distortions obscuring our understandings of shared histories.

Useful starting points can begin with the following:

1. A paradigm that can help to surface some of the hidden formative factors in our belief systems is the *decolonizing self-scrutiny.*

We begin transforming our perceptions and practices by examining our personal history with a critical awareness of its defining factors. Identifying and assessing the colonizing process, which has impacted all of us, is an important part of our evolution. We can ask ourselves the following questions:

- *How might I describe my past before I was aware of biases?*
- *How did I interact with people who belong to a different 'class' than myself, or who looked or thought differently than I was familiar with?*
- *What was the impact of my behaviours at spiritual, physical, and emotional levels on these people?*
- *How has that impact been passed on to others?*
- *What is the impact of this history on me?*

Building on these questions of self-investigation, "Another way that inclusive practice may be established is to stress the importance of both acknowledging fears and anxieties and of speaking from one's own experiences. A working assumption may be that inequality affects everyone, and dealing with the impact of oppression is a lifelong process, one with which the educator, too, is still engaged." (Wane, 2007: 17)

Those who have benefitted from colonial and imperialist adventures and acquisitions can add the questions:

- *What is my family history in the European conquest of the world?*
- *What benefits have accrued to my generation and to me as an individual?*
- *What deprivations have I experienced as a result of this history?*

2. In a workshop on 'Decolonizing the Self', authors Dempsey and O[i] identify the numerous "colonial systems and ideologies [that] persist

---

i Olive Dempsey and Debora O (2003), 'Decolonizing the SELF'.

in our modern worlds and particularly in our everyday lives. They act as devices of control that manipulate how we perceive our rights and our agency." They also observe that "[D]ecolonization requires that both the colonized and the colonizer come to terms with the insidious ways in which ideologies of colonialism have permeated most aspects of our daily lives, both there and here, then and now."

We can approach the task from an individual standpoint, adding to our understanding of social location by answering the question: *How do I come to be here, on this land?*

When we are presented with information, we can assess it critically by asking the following questions:

- *Who is sending out this information?*
- *Is anyone hurt by this information?*
- *Whose voices are ignored or marginalized in this information?*
- *Who stands to benefit from the dissemination of this information?*
- *Is this information the total story?*

By critically examining the information we receive, whether through the media or during the rigors of academic pursuit, we develop our intellectual processing facilities, in effect *decolonizing* and liberating our minds from absorbing false or misleading information and automatically processing it as *the* truth. We become aware that historical and contemporary realities are multi-faceted, each with its layers of complexity. As educators we must interrogate these complexities and free ourselves from cognitive insularity.

3. Lawrence and Dua (2005: 137) suggest that the academy review prevailing assumptions and accept the Aboriginal perspective in three areas:

Aboriginal sovereignty: This is assumed to be more of a principle in theory than a legitimate and reachable goal. But in reality Indigenous communities have been working and organizing for sovereignty for many years.

Knowledge Construction: Understand the *centrality* of "ongoing colonization to the construction of knowledge about race and racism."

Indigenous Issues: Include Indigenous issues in antiracist activism in ways that do not marginalize and disempower Indigenous peoples.

SECTION TWO

EXERCISES

INDIVIDUAL SELF-ASSESSMENT

Effecting any change in ourselves requires a clear understanding of where we stand when beginning the process of transformation. The exercises in this section offer some tools toward self-reflection and (beginning) self-transformation.

VALUES DEVELOPMENT

The social location exercise is one in which we consciously identify where we are placed in our social, cultural and political landscape. The exercises in this section are guides to developing an awareness of our social location and the values we have internalized as part of the socialization process.

SOCIAL LOCATION EXERCISE 1: *The Family Flower*

On each petal, write a value you have learned within your family setting.

Examine the values that are part of your Family Flower and ask yourself the following questions about each:

- *When did I learn this?*

- *What does it mean?*

- *What are its implications?*

- *Is it a value I practice often, sometimes, rarely?*

- *Is it a value I want to keep?*

- *What would I have to do to develop new values?*

SOCIAL LOCATION EXERCISE 2: *The Collective Garden*

We have had concepts and beliefs related to other peoples, other ethnic groups, and other races implanted in our individual and collective consciousness. These beliefs constitute a 'garden' of socio-cultural norms.

Name some of the commonly-held collective beliefs you have inherited from your community culture.

- *How have these beliefs manifested in your behaviour with interracial contacts?*

- *Do you hold certain beliefs but conceal them in an effort to be "politically correct?"*

- *What collective beliefs do others within your community or social sphere share in regard to racialization?*

- *How have these impacted you?*

- *Do these beliefs affect your relationship with others in your community or social sphere?*

SOCIAL LOCATION EXERCISE 3: *The National and Personal Forest*

Some of the most powerful trees in the fertile ground of our consciousness have been planted and tended by institutions of the state – educational, governmental, public services – and private satellites such as the media and entertainment industries. These trees constitute a national *and* personal forest of our beliefs, are often difficult to identify, and once identified, difficult to uproot.

Name the 'belief' trees in the National forest. Name those in your 'personal' forest. *To what extent are they similar? To what extent do they diverge?*

- *How did they get there?*
- *Why are they still there?*
- *Do you see any that need to be uprooted?*
- *What steps could be taken to uproot them?*
- *Can you think of trees that could replace them?*

Name the trees you see in your own forest.
- *How did they get there?*
- *Do you see any trees that should be uprooted?*
- *What can you see when you look past them?*
- *What would happen if you started to uproot some of them?*
- *What can you see when you uproot these trees?*

POWER LINES EXERCISE 1: *Power*

What is our relation to power? What role does power play in society? Understanding power and our own relationship to it is crucial.

1. <u>What *is* power?</u>

Write down your responses in the form of a mind map as illustrated below:

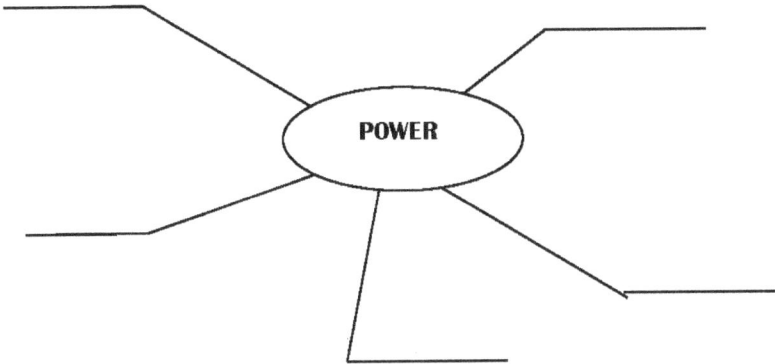

POWER

2. <u>Identify a form of power that *you* have.</u> Mind map it as above, with the keyword at the centre. *What does this power enable you to do? How does this power enable your access, advancement, social standing? How does this power make you feel about yourself and your place in the world? How does this power make you feel about others who do not have this power?*

3. <u>Identify a form of power that you *don't have.*</u> Mind map as before, with the keyword at the centre. *What does this lack of specific power prevent you from doing? What does it prevent you from having? What does it prevent you from being? How does the lack of this specific power make you feel about yourself? Does it affect your access, advancement, social standing?*

Note: In this particular exercise, if one's primary modes are didactic, they might challenge themselves to change their practice.

POWER LINES EXERCISE 2: *Role Playing*

Role playing is an effective tool for acquiring an understanding of other positions, perceptions, and worldviews. It can be instrumental in surfacing our own **actual** positions, perceptions and assumptions.

The following exercise in role play continues our work toward **understanding our relations to power.**

Observation and commentary should be open and aware. Be mindful of the ground rules of

- **respect**
- **sensitivity to self**
- **sensitivity to other**
- **remaining within the collectively established vocabularies and analysis.**

ROLEPLAY

Characters: A teenager, a parent, a teacher.

Situation: The youth has been accused of plagiarizing an essay. The parent has come to discuss the issue with the teacher.

Instructions: In groups of 6, enact the discussion.

Three people do the role playing

Three observe and comment afterwards

Then do it again, switching roles: the person who played the parent, now plays the youth; and the person who represented the teacher, now becomes the parent

The movement between roles is very elucidating, and the exercise can be usefully repeated a third time with a further switch in roles where the teacher plays the student; the student plays the parent, and the parent plays the teacher. Use any other variations that occur to you or others in the group.

POWER LINES EXERCISE 3: *Images*

Instructor's notes:

1.   Prepare a collage of at least a half-dozen magazines distributed via the typical news stands at supermarkets. They will vary depending on the target consumer population of each supermarket. It will be illuminating to have more than one collage, showing the kinds of images the magazine publishers consider to be those acceptable to the targeted consumer.

2.   Give participants time to examine the images without commentary.

3.   Have each person quickly write down their thoughts, reactions, and associations randomly and without any attempt to order or doctor them.

4.   Open the discussion and pose the following questions:

Questions
- *Who is the target consumer?*
- *What are the assumed characteristics of the consumer?*
- *What do the images tell you?*
- *What message/s are the images conveying?*
- *What does the image seek to elicit from the viewer/reader?*

Enable the group to comfortably discuss the images. However, some individuals may be uncomfortable or hesitant about revealing or discussing responses to some questions. It is not necessary to challenge them to do so. The viewpoints and understandings generated in the group will affect everyone, but there may not necessarily be a free and open discussion.

SECTION THREE

RAISING OUR AWARENESS

The Blind Seer Exercise Part I

Instructors Notes:
These exercises have the potential to unseat some of our unconscious and, therefore, most stubborn assumptions. Instructors should lead participants with this in mind. Allow ample time at each stage and exercise. Be aware of each person and attentive to what he or she is experiencing. Do the exercises one at a time with structured breaks between them.

Materials:
- 10 long sashes of different colours, with one end of each sash fixed to a standing holder strong enough to remain in place.
- Flipcharts

PROCEDURE:
1. Organize the seating in a circle. At the centre of the circle fix the sashes holder.

2   With all the participants seated, lead a sash to each one. At the beginning they just hold on to them.

3   Ask each person to say what attributes they associate with the colour they hold. Don't prompt. If someone makes no associations with the colour, others can supply them. This is how social constructing works!
Once a set of attributes has been verbalized, whether by the person himself/herself or others —and recorded on the flipcharts—that person's character is identified with those attributes.

4   Give time for each person to internalize the concept, and what it means for them. *They are expected to conform to the attributes of the colour they have been assigned.*

This exercise allows people to enter into a conscious experiencing of the function and force of social judgments, assumptions, and expectations.

Stereotyping is a mechanism of social/class control and population manipulation. Think of the ethnic or racial, and national or religious stereotypes *you* hold about Jews, Africans, Caucasians, Native Americans, First Nations, Chinese, Japanese, Europeans, French, Muslims, Russians, Blacks, Whites, Christians, Mormons, Catholics, Palestinians, etc.

Some stereotypes are positive, some are negative, but all have notable social impacts. We are all "coloured" by the social and politically constructed definitions and labels of others. How many stereotypical constructs of 'others' can you recall? Which groups have mostly positive stereotypes? Which groups have mostly negative stereotypes? What is the difference in regard to disadvantaged groups versus advantaged groups?

- *How did you feel within your colour definition?*
- *What effect did it have on your sense of self?*
- *What would happen if you refused the definition determined by others?*

The Blind Seer Exercise Part 2

With the participants still sitting, have them wrap the sash over their eyes and try to look around through the fabric. Ask each participant the following questions:

Questions
- *What effect does the "veil" have on your viewpoint?*
- *What implications do you see for these effects?*

The Blind Seer Exercise Part 3

Materials:
- A range of colour markers
- Individual sheets for each colour, listing the attributes and associations assigned to that colour by prevailing custom (*These information sheets should not be available to the participants before the Part 2 exercise*).

INSTRUCTIONS

Give out sheets and colour markers and ask everyone to trace one of their hands and then colour it in with their colour (i.e., whichever colour they've been given).

While they are tracing and colouring their hand, ask them to think deeply about what it means for them to be that colour.

Say to them: "This is the colour that other people assign to you; it is, therefore, the colour that you are; it has fixed, generally accepted attributes and you are expected to conform to those attributes. This is the life you've been given," or "this is the life that's been decided for you."

- *What are the implications, for you, of this categorization?*
- *How do you feel about this?*
- *What does your future look like?*
- *Your past?*
- *Your present?*

COMMON GROUND EXERCISE [i]

PROCEDURE:

1. Ask participants to arrange themselves in a circle where everyone has room to step forward.
2. Read out the statements below and ask participants to step forward if they feel they identify with the statement being read.
3. After reading each statement, ask participants to look around and observe who has stepped forward and who has not. Reform the circle after each statement.
4. When the list of statements has been exhausted, ask group members to volunteer statements of group identifications that apply to their particular age or community grouping.
5. When debriefing, ask volunteers to say how they felt when they stepped forward. Did they feel alienated, isolated, pressured to step forward, embarrassed, or any other feelings they experienced.

---

[i] Adapted from student project, 'Anti-Racist Education Studies' EDU5510, Wane (2006)

I am a woman

I am a man

I am a teacher

I am scared about the future

I have felt judged because of the way I look

I feel comfortable in a community of people with the same religion as my own

I come from a middle-class background

I feel comfortable in a community of homosexuals

I have felt rejected because of the colour of my skin

I feel comfortable in a community of people with disabilities

I come from a family of two parents

I feel comfortable in a community of people for whom English is not their first language

I have felt rejected because of somebody that I loved

I have felt rejected because of my body size

I have an alcoholic parent

I am an immigrant to Canada

I know someone who has been affected by AIDS

I know someone who has committed suicide

There is something in my life I regret and would take back if given the opportunity

Some of the above statements were true for me but I chose not to step forward

SECTION FOUR

INSTITUTIONAL ASSESSMENT

Two tools are suggested here to begin the work of assessing the organization you are working with.

Checklist

In trying to understand the role of the institution in fostering or hindering racial equity the following checklist can be a useful tool.

Do entrance requirements acknowledge prior learning/experience/skills?	
Are communications available in languages consistent with its user populations?	
Is testing done in languages consistent with its user populations?	
Is it culturally accessible? (i.e., are there visible members of user groups on staff? Are institutional representatives trained in multicultural competencies? Are there initial contacts with sensitized staff who visibly represent racial groups other than the dominant one?	
Is the paperwork in plain language?	
Do promotional materials include images of people of colour? In proportion to their population percentage?	
Are images employed in print and electronic communications to facilitate cross lingual accessibility?	
Do the images include styles and representations that have cross-cultural meaning?	

Who is in the leadership roles? (including management team, board, advisors)	
What are the institutional priorities with regard to racial issues? Have statements and policies been produced? If not, what process is in place?	
Is there an accessible, culturally-sensitive process in place for complaints?	
Is there a track record of responding to complaints in a timely and constructive manner?	
What structures are there for facilitating community involvement in institutional development, growth, changes?	
Does community input affect policies, decisions, structures of the organization?	

IDENTIFYING ORGANIZATIONAL CULTURE

Answers to the following questions can reveal a picture of the cultural norms that you encounter in an organization – ie: "cultural mapping."[i] They can generate insight into the internal identity of the group, institution, or department and provide an important starting point for any plan of change.

Questions

- Who are the representatives of the institution? What do they look like? Do they have characteristic ways of dressing, of interacting with each other and across affiliations? Is their style informal, professional, frank or tactful?
- Who are the 'insiders' in this organization? Who are the 'outsiders'?
- Can you identify any characteristic vocabulary?
- What are the formal and informal norms of decision-making?
- How does the organization customarily handle conflict?

Note: Add your own questions based on your experience or knowledge of the organization.

---

i *Adapted from Arnold et al. (1991). Educating For A Change, pp. 16-18.*

"We now live in a diverse, postmodern, ever-evolving society. As always, race and social class are inextricably linked together. The public education system has to be a major player in the transformation of Canada into a much more inclusive and positive society for all people. After all, it was one of the crucial instruments for maintaining white hegemony, and it may very well still be. For the most part the education system works to maintain corporate hegemony today. Anti-racist education, of course, is the first step in the transformation."

Paul Orlowski, 'Ties That Bind and Ties That Blind: Race and Class Intersections in the Classroom', in (eds.) Carl E. James and Adrienne Shadd, *Talking about Identity: Encounters in Race, Ethnicity, and Language* (2001: 266)

SOURCES

About Canada: Multiculturalism in Canada. http://www.mta.ca/faculty/arts/canadian_studies/ english/abaout/multi/indeed.htm

Ani, Marimba. (1994. Yurugu: An African-Centered Critique of European Cultural Thought and Behavior. Africa World Press Inc. Trenton.

Appiah, K. Anthony and Amy Gutmann (1996). Color Conscious: The Political Morality of Race. Princeton University Press.

Applebaum, Herbert (1987. (ed) Perspectives in Cultural Anthropology

Arnold, Rick, Bev Burke, Carl James, D'Arcy Martin, Barb Thomas (1991). Educating For A Change. Between the Lines and the Doris Marshall Institute for Education and Action, Toronto.

Beck et al. (1997). The Sacred: Ways *of Knowledge, Sources of Life.* The Navajo Community College Press. Arizona

Bonnett, Alastair and Bruce Carrington (1996). "Constructions Of Anti-racist Education in Britain and Canada." Comparative Education, 32:3, 271-288.

Calliste, Agnes and George Dei, eds. (2000). Anti-Racist Feminism: Critical Race and Gender Studies. Fernwood Publishing, Halifax.

Canadian Race Relations Foundation. Website, accessed April 2007 http://www.crr.ca/Load.do?section=26&subSection=37&id=234&type=2

Carrington, Bruce and Alastair Bonnett (1997). "The Other Canadian "Mosaic;" "Race' Equity Education in Ontario and British Columbia." Comparative Education 33:3, 411-431.

Case, Frederick Ivor (2002). Racism & National Consciousness. New and revised edition. Other Eye: Toronto

Churchill, Ward (*October 28 2006). Lecture at New College, University of Toronto, Conference on Racism and National Consciousness, "National Security and the Treatment of Difference."

Davis, Angela (1983). Women, Race and Class. Vintage Books, New York

Dei, George (1995). "Integrative Anti-Racism: Intersection of Race, Class and Gender." Race, Gender and Class 2:3, 11-30.

Dei et al. (1997). Reconstructing 'Drop-Out': A Critical Ethnography Of The Dynamics of Black Students' Disengagement From School.

University of Toronto Press

Dei, George and Gurpreet Johal, eds. (2005). Antiracist Research Methodologies. Peter Lang   Publishing, New York

Dempsey, Olive and Debora O 2003 "Decolonising the SELF." E. Peak Features, 10:113,   March 10, 2003. http://www.peak.sfu.ca/the-peak/2003-1/issue10/fe-decolself.html

Dewing, Michael, Leman, Marc. "Canadian Multiculturalism." Political and Social Affairs   Division, Parliamentary Information and Research Service, Revised 16 March 2006.

Disability Statistics Canada, posted in Facts and Statistics by Stats Canada. Website: http://www.disabled-world.com/disability/statistics/disability-statistics-canada_printer.php   accessed 5/1/2009

Disability Facts and Statistics. http//www.disabled-world.com/disability/statistics accessed   5/1/2009

Fanon, Frantz (1967: 18). Black Skin, White Masks (translated from the French by Charles Lam   Markmann). Grove Press. New York

Frideres, James S., Gadacz, Rene R (1943). Aboriginal Peoples in Canada. Pearson/Prentice   Hall. Toronto

Fellows, Mary Louise and Sherene Razack (1998). "The Race to Innocence: Confronting   Hierarchical Relations among Women." The Journal of Gender, Race and Justice 1:2.

Goldstein, Richard (1984). In (ed.) Quincy Troupe, James Baldwin: The Legacy (1989: 177)

Graveline, Fyre Jean (1998). Circle Works: Transforming Eurocentric Consciousness. Fernwood   Publishing, Halifax.

Hamalengwa, Munyonzwe. "The Role of the Judiciary in Racial Profiling: A Case Study of   Canada. Website: http://www.isrl.ora/Papers/Davies.pdf (accessed 2 May 2009)

Hart, Mechthild (1985). "Thematization of power, the search for common interests, and self- reflection: Towards   a   comprehensive concept of emancipatory education," International

Journal of Lifelong Education 4:2 119 – 134. http://simplelink.library.utoronto.ca/url.cfm/28087

Henry, Frances (1995). "Racism Revisited In 'Toronto The Good.' " Currents, 8:3, 12-15.

Hightower-Langston, Donna. (2003). The Native American World. John Wiley & Sons.   Hoboken. New Jersey hooks, bell Killing Rage:Ending Racism1995. Henry Holt and Company, NY.

Ighodaro, MacDonald E. (2006). Living the Experience: Migration, Exclusion and Anti-Racist Practice, Fernwood Publishing, Halifax.

James, Royson (2009). In "Toronto's diversity not as perfect as we think". Toronto Star GT2. 12 March 2009.

Karpinski, Eva C. (ed.). Pens of Many Colours: A Canadian Reader (Second Edition). Harcourt Canada Ltd. (1997)

Lawrence, Bonita (2003). "Gender, Race, and the Regulation of Native Identity in Canada and the United States: An Overview"Hypatia 18.2 3(31). http://simplelink.library.utoronto.ca/url.cfm/28088.

Lawrence, Bonita and Enakshi Dua (2005). "Decolonising AntiRacism." Social Justice: A Journal of Crime, Conflict and World Order 32: 4 120(24).

Lee, Enid, "The Anti-Racism Lens." Website, accessed April 2007. http://www.enidlee.com/,

Locker, Kitty O., Findlay, Isabel M. Business Communication Now (Canadian Edition), McGraw-Hill Ryerson (2009) a subsidiary of McGraw Hill Inc.

Lopes, Tina and Barb Thomas (2006). Dancing On Live Embers: Challenging Racism in Organizations. Between the Lines, Toronto.

Mansfield, Earl and John Kehoe (1994). "A Critical Examination Of Anti-Racist Education." Canadian Journal of Education 19: 4, 418-430.

Martin, Judith N., Nakayama, Thomas K. Intercultural Communication In Contexts (Fourth Edition) McGraw-Hill, an imprint of the McGraw-Hill Companies, Inc. Avenue of the Americas. New York, N.Y.

McCaskell, Tim (2005). Race to Equity: Disrupting Educational Inequality. Between the Lines, Toronto.

McClester, Cedric. Kwanzaa: Everything You Always Wanted To Know But Didn't Know But Didn't Know Where To Ask (revised edition). Gumbs & Thomas. New York

McIntosh, Peggy (1988). "White Privilege: Unpacking the Invisible Knapsack." Independent Schools Winter 1990.

Mensah, Joseph (2002). Black Canadians: history, experiences, social conditions. Fernwood Publishing. Halifax

Moodley, Kogila (2003). "Understanding the Forms and Functions of Racism; Toward the Development of Promising Practices." Education Canada 40:1, 44-50.

Multiculturalism in Canada: A Study of the subject by Mount Allison University, Presenting Immigration, Policy, Attitudes, Racial and Ethnic Diversity and the Future. Retrieved on

July 10, 2009 from website http://www.mta.ca/about_Canada/multi/

Native Women's Association of Canada. "Number of Aboriginal People in Canada's Prisons Growing." Report released 16 October 2006. website: http://www.afn.ca/cmslib/ general/NAOs.pdf (accessed 1 May 2009)

Native Women's Association of Canada. "Aboriginal Women and the Legal Justice System in Canada: An Issue Paper. Prepared for the National Aboriginal Women's Summit, June 20-22, 2007 in Corner Brook, NL. Website: http://www.nwac-hq.org/en/documents/ nwac-legal.pdf (accessed 1 May 2009)

Ontario's Equity And Inclusive Education Strategy: Revitalizing the Promise of Diversity (2009)

Pieterse, Jan, Parekh, Bhikhu (eds.) The Decolonization of Imagination: Culture, Knowledge and

Power. Zed Books: London and New Jersey (1991)

Portrait of the Canadian Population in 2006, 2006 Census – Statistics Canada – Catalogue no. 97-550

Raby, Rebecca (2004). "There's no racism at my school, it's just joking around: ramifications for anti-racist education." Race Ethnicity and Education, 7:4, 367-383.

Radcliffe-Brown, "On Social Structure," in (ed.) Herbert Applebaum (1987: 128). Perspectives in Cultural Anthropology. State University of New York Press

Raptis, Helen and Thomas Fleming (1998) "Unravelling Multicultural Education's Meanings: Analysis of Core Assumptions Found In Academic Writings in Canada and the Canada and United States, 1981-1997." Journal of Educational Thought 32:2, 169-94.

Shelton, Antoni (1995). "Race Relations In Canada: A Troubled Past and Strained Future." Currents, 8:3, 8-11.

Smith, Charles (2007). Conflict, Crisis, and Accountability: Racial Profiling and Law Enforcement in Canada. Canadian Centre For Policy Alternatives, Ottawa.

Suderman, Jane. Understanding Intercultural Communication (Thomson/Nelson – Nelson, a division of Thomson Canada Limited (2007)

The Native Americans: An Illustrated History. (Ed.) Alvin M. Joseph, Jr. Turner Publishing Inc. (1993)

Volgyi, Bistra-Beatrix (2006). "Integrative Anti-Racism Education: Discourse and Practice," Unpublished paper.

Wane, Njoki (2006). "Is Decolonization Possible." In Anti-Colonialism and Education: The Politics of Resistance, eds George Dei and Arlo Kempf, Sense Publishers.

Wane, Njoki (2007). "Contested Site, Contested Topic: Teaching Diversity in a Teacher Education Program." Unpublished paper.

Winks, Robin W. The Blacks in Canada: A History (Second Edition). McGill University Press (1997)

APPENDIX "A"
Immigration: The Early Years

NOTE: The following, 'Immigration: The Early Years' is taken from *About Canada: Multiculturalism in Canada.*, and can be found on the website:

http://www.mta.ca/faculty/arts/canadian_studies/english/about/multi/index.htm

The *About Canada* publication "is a series of brief analytical overviews of modern Canadian issues, and culture...produced by the Centre for Canadian Studies at Mount Allison University in cooperation with **Canadian Heritage Canadian Studies Programme.** These issues were designed and published between 1993-1997, and are prepared by faculty with appropriate expertise from universities across Canada." The editor is Joanne Goodrich.

Immigration: The Early Years

Immigration has played and continues to play a key role in shaping the character of Canadian society. Although only a minority of Canadians have first-hand experience of immigration, all Canadians have a parent, grandparent or more distant relative who came to Canada as a stranger in a strange land. Because all Canadians share an immigrant past, there would be no Canada without immigration.

Tens of thousands of years before the coming of the first European settlers, ancestors of Canada's Native People migrated across a frozen icepack linking Asia to North America. Over many centuries they spread across the continent, forming a rich tapestry of cultural and linguistic groupings. Approximately 500 years ago, Europeans arrived in what would eventually become Canada. First came French colonists who carved out homes along the St. Lawrence River and its tributaries. They were followed by settlers from France and Britain who gradually established competing colonial outposts in the Maritime provinces. The 18th century victory of British arms at Quebec, followed by the British defeat in the American Revolution sent Loyalists northward to British North America (Canada) in search of new homes.

During most of the next century and a half, immigration continued. Settlers came mainly from Britain, including English, Scots and Irish. Some were drawn to the opportunities of the new world. Others, including many Scots and Irish famine immigrants, escaped the grinding poverty and starvation which followed crop failures or eviction from their lands. Americans also immigrated. Many were lured north to Canada by Canadian land agents or labour recruiters. Some immigrants came empty-handed and alone. Others came in family groups and with the resources necessary to begin life afresh in a new land. Some succeeded, while others struggled and reaped only misery.

While the majority of early immigrants came to Canada from Britain or the United States, other nationalities also came, including non-whites. Many immigrants from continental Europe were drawn to Canada by its economic promise, or as an escape from religious or political threats. In the years before the American Civil War, the Europeans were joined by thousands of black slaves who escaped by following the Underground Railway northward into Canada. After Canadian Confederation in 1867, thousands of Irish and Chinese labourers were imported as workers to build the Canadian Pacific Railway. On the Pacific coast, other Chinese joined the rush of fortune hunters from all over the world who trekked into British Columbia and later the Yukon interior after the discovery of gold.

After the turn of the century, hundreds of thousands of American farmers moved northward into the Canadian prairies in search of farm lands. At the same time, many from central and eastern Europe, seeking land, were recruited by Canadian immigration agents anxious to fill the west with farmers.

While Canada's western lands filled with settlers, other newcomers laboured in Canada's expanding lumber, mining, railway, manufacturing and construction industries. Some planned to stay and become Canadians; others wished only to save money and then return to their families. Meanwhile, the money these sojourners sent home helped support those who remained behind. But whatever their motives for coming to Canada and whether or not they ended up staying permanently, each newcomer played a role in the building of Canada.

www.ingramcontent.com/pod-product-compliance
Lightning Source LLC
Chambersburg PA
CBHW030735280326
41926CB00086B/1652

* 9 7 8 1 9 2 6 9 0 6 2 0 1 *